Tanzania: The Land, Its People and Contemporary Life

David Lawrence

1

Tanzania: The Land, Its People and Contemporary Life
David Lawrence

First Edition

ISBN 978-9987-9308-3-8

New Africa Press
Dar es Salaam, Tanzania

Contents

Chapter Five:
The People of Tanzania
and Their Ethnic Identities

Chapter Six:
The Union of Tanganyika
and Zanzibar

Appendix I:
Tanganyika Before Independence

Appendix II:
The Swahili People
and Swahili Culture

Appendix III:
Tanzania in A Capsule

Appendix IV:
Nyerere and Nkrumah on Continental
Union under one Government

Introduction

THIS book is a general introduction to Tanzania. It's intended for those who are going to Tanzania for the first time and for anybody else who wants to learn some basic facts about the largest country in East Africa.

The country has a rich history. In fact, if it existed as a nation throughout the centuries when the people in this part of Africa interacted with other cultures and continents as they still do today, it would be one of the oldest countries and nations in the world.

Tanzania also has one of the largest numbers of ethnic groups in Africa together with only a handful of other countries. In fact, only four countries on the entire continent have more than 100 tribes or ethnic groups. Tanzania is one of them.

Readers are going to learn quite a few things about those tribes and where they live in Tanzania.

Also covered in the book are the towns and cities in all the provinces of this large country.

Tanzania also is unique in one fundamental respect. It's

the only union of two independent countries ever formed on the continent. And it's the only one that exists today almost half a century after it was formed.

The union between Tanganyika and Zanzibar is one of the subjects covered in the book, and readers are going to learn about one of the most important events in the history of post-colonial Africa on a continent where the quest for unity has remained an elusive dream since independence in the fifties and sixties.

The book also includes a lot of information on Tanganyika just before independence and how it became one of the first countries in Africa to emerge from colonial rule.

Also included is some material on one of the most interesting ethnic groups in African history and how it came into being.

They are the Swahili whose language is also known as Swahili especially among many people around the world who are not native speakers of the language. Among the native speakers, the language is called Kiswahili.

It's the main language spoken in Tanzania and Kenya. It's also spoken in several other countries in east-central Africa. And we are going to learn something about this language which transcends ethnicity.

Kiswahili is not identified with any African tribe, making it a truly Pan-African language building bridges across ethnicity, cultures and nations especially in the eastern part of the continent.

And as you learn about Tanzania, you are also going to learn a few things about an area bigger than Tanzania because of the country's connection to other parts of East Africa and beyond.

Welcome to Tanzania. And welcome to Africa.

Chapter One:

Tanzania:
A Panoramic View

TANZANIA is the largest country in East Africa and one of the largest on the continent in terms of area and population.

It is, in fact, one of the largest countries in the world and ranks 31st among all the countries in terms of area. It's 378,000 square miles and is somewhat bigger than Nigeria but much smaller in terms of population. Tanzania has about 40 million people and Nigeria about 140 million.

The former island nation of Zanzibar, now part of Tanzania, has an area of 640 square miles and a population of about 600,000.

Tanzania also is the size of Texas, Oklahoma and West Virginia combined or slightly more than twice the size of California.

It's bordered by Kenya and Uganda on the north, Rwanda and Burundi on the northwest, the Democratic Republic of Congo (DRC) on the west, by Zambia and Malawi on the southwest, Mozambique on the south, and by the Indian Ocean on the east.

It became one country when Tanganyika united with Zanzibar on 26 April 1964.

When the two countries united, the new country was known as the United Republic of Tanganyika and Zanzibar. Its name was changed on 29 October the same year when it became the United Republic of Tanzania. But the most commonly used name is Tanzania.

Tanganyika won independence on 9 December 1961, and Zanzibar on 10 December 1963 but with little legitimacy since the black African majority was excluded from power by the ruling Arab minority; an injustice which triggered the Zanzibar revolution on 12 January 1964. Both countries won independence from Britain.

Not long after Tanganyika won independence under the leadership of Julius Nyerere, the government formulated the policy of *ujamaa*, Nyerere's African version of socialism. It also introduced one-party rule.

The first two decades after independence were a critical period in the history of the country in terms of political and economic transformation.

Many changes took place in the economic and political arena, and their impact on the nation still reverberates today across the spectrum. As Edwin Mtei, former governor of the Bank of Tanzania who also once served as minister of finance under Nyerere and as the last secretary-general of the first East African Community (EAC) which collapsed in 1977, stated years later in an interview published on 17 January 2005 in *The East African*:

"You were the first governor of the Bank of Tanzania, which is believed to have struck the first blow to the former East African Community

prompting the demise of the East African Currency Board - which had ensured the strength of the common currency, and thus the common market. You were also minister for finance during the early 1970s, the years of the Arusha Declaration. Both positions made you responsible for the country's economic performance. How would you describe this period?

I should start by clarifying my own involvement in these matters.

I was appointed permanent secretary to the Treasury in August 1964. In this capacity I was the Tanzania member of the East African Currency Board.

Its chairman was the secretary-general of the East African Common Services Organisation. The other members were my counterparts in Kenya, Uganda and the Aden Protectorate (now South Yemen). Another member was provided by the Bank of England and served as our technical adviser.

Early in 1965, the governments of Tanzania, Kenya and Uganda realised that they would not be establishing a political federation in the foreseeable future. Had the federation materialised, the Board would have been transformed into the federal central bank.

The three governments then agreed to establish separate central banks and currencies and to break up the East African Currency Board.

Being the permanent secretary for finance, I found myself recruiting experts in central banking and arranging the training of local personnel who later joined the Bank of Tanzania. My own career changed drastically when President Julius Nyerere appointed me governor-designate of the Bank of Tanzania in October 1965.

From then onwards, I devoted my efforts to preparing the legislation for the bank, the national currency and all the other prerequisites, so that the Bank of Tanzania was able to issue the national currency by June 14, 1966.

Uganda and Kenya followed suit soon afterwards, so that by October 1966 the East African Currency Board had ceased to function.

True, the East African shilling was a strong currency. But this was because the partner states' fiscal policies then were cautious and non-inflationary, and this stance had nothing to do with the EACB. Besides, the continuation of the common market could not be attributed to the strength or the commonness of the currency.

The common market lasted because the partner states wanted it to last and, indeed, it continued to operate for 10 years after the demise of the common currency and the currency board.

I also do not think that currencies in a common market have all to be strong.

The important thing is that there must be agreed rates of exchange and the partners in the market must be ready to trade freely without restrictions.

When the Arusha Declaration was being drafted, I was invited only as an observer at the meeting of Tanu, which was held in Arusha at the end of January 1967. As governor of the central bank I could not have influenced the decisions made there.

Another point is that my appointment as minister for finance and planning was more than 10 years later, in mid-February 1977, when the president recalled me from the East African Community.

The EAC was then collapsing following Nyerere's decision to close the Kenya-Tanzania border earlier that month.

One could say that it was from then only that I could seriously be regarded as a participant in economic policy making in Tanzania.

What was the economic situation like during Nyerere's administration - under which you served - as against that under Hassan Mwinyi; and Mwinyi's in

contrast to the current one of Benjamin Mkapa?

The Nyerere regime lasted for 24 years [1961-1985], and one can identify several phases in the evolution of the economy of Tanzania over this period.

The first phase ended with the promulgation of the Arusha Declaration in February 1967.

During the struggle for independence, Tanu had undertaken to rid Tanganyika of poverty, ignorance and disease, as the people's expectations were high at the time of independence.

The British government had agreed to only modest financial assistance to Tanganyika during the independence negotiations and the bulk of that aid was paid to the departing British colonial civil servants as compensation for redundancies.

The country was dependent basically on peasant agriculture for staple food. The exports were sisal, coffee and cotton. Diamonds also figured as a substantial part of Tanganyika's exports.

When the Union came into being in 1964, cloves from Zanzibar became one of the major exports of Tanzania. The first development plan, of three years, was drawn up with these modest resources and that was when Nyerere coined the phrase 'Kupanga ni Kuchagua (Planning is Choosing [your future]).'

The national motto at that time was Uhuru ni Kazi (Freedom is Hard Work).

In that development plan we started pilot projects of Integrated Development Villages and I recall taking foreign dignitaries to Upper Kitete near Lake Manyara as a showpiece of what could be done under the "integrated" approach.

Most of the public funds were spent on the intensive training programme for the Africanisation of the civil service, building of schools and hospitals.

The frustrating pace occasioned by inadequate flow of

financial resources for development, I guess, made Nyerere opt for the Arusha Declaration hoping that it would be a faster and fairer way to development.

On the promulgation of the Declaration, the second phase of the Nyerere era began. The nationalisation of banks, insurance companies, major manufacturing and trading firms and sisal estates followed immediately. Uncertainties on the part of owners of substantial assets in the country caused a massive flight of capital and we had to introduce strict exchange controls.

The government also embarked on many new projects of manufacturing, especially in the textile sector. In the tourist sector, hotels and tourist lodges were built in the national parks.

By the end of 1969, most of the negotiations for compensation for nationalised assets had been completed, confidence had returned and we were able to relax exchange controls.

However, in 1971, further drastic measures were taken when all large residential and business buildings were nationalised.

The majority of the owners affected were members of the Asian urban community, and the panic that ensued saw a large number of them emigrating, especially to India, Pakistan, the UK and Canada.

It was again necessary to prevent excessive depletion of our foreign reserves and so strict exchange controls were reintroduced.

This was also during the construction of the Tanzania-Zambia Railway (Tazara) by the Chinese government.

The arrangement was that China would supply Tanzania and Zambia Chinese-made consumer goods without demanding immediate payment.

These goods were sold by the importing parastatals and the local currency generated was paid to Tazara to use for the construction, the value of these consumer goods figuring as part of the long-term loan by China.

In this way the market was flooded with Chinese goods and in spite of complaints from local and East African Common Market manufacturers of competing materials, Tanzanian consumers were satisfied.

The third phase of the Nyerere era began about 1972/73, when the government started to implement the Ujamaa village programme.

People were relocated from their ancestral land to new areas, which were planned as communal villages.

These ujamaa villages were designed to have basic social amenities like schools, hospitals, social halls or community centres and water supply. Each family in the village was allotted a parcel of land to grow food or other crops of their own choice; but there was also a large parcel of land earmarked for the whole village for communal farming.

The scheme had started by persuading the people and explaining the advantages of relocation. However, when it came to moving people with perennial crops or with permanent houses, there was resistance. Overenthusiastic officials began to apply force to move people; some houses were even burnt down.

A large proportion of the population of Tanzania suddenly found itself building shelters in the new locations. It then became necessary to feed the new arrivals and a lot of public funds were expended for food. The season for preparing the land to grow crops passed without a large number of peasants doing their normal work because of their preoccupation with building new houses or shelters. Large tracts of land lay fallow.

Unfortunately, the period of relocation coincided with the severe drought of 1973/74. The famine that followed was therefore devastating. Tanzania found itself without adequate food and was compelled to import large amounts of food to prevent widespread starvation.

Friendly countries gave us food as aid and we even had to import food from countries which were not friendly.

Our reserves of foreign exchange dropped to rock bottom and we began to experience difficulties in meeting repayment of contractual debts.

It was at this time that as a nation we started experiencing negative gross domestic growth.

The non-performance of many of the parastatals set up as a result of the Arusha Declaration also began at this time. Many were under-capitalised, others lacked proper management, while others, especially those involved in manufacturing, were supplied of faulty, over-valued or inappropriate machinery.

The Treasury found itself either giving huge loans to these firms to rescue their management from irate employees who had gone without salaries for long periods or for repaying loans as guarantors since the borrowing parastatals were not generating the necessary surpluses. Factories under construction were left uncompleted, equipment delivered for installation was either faulty or lay rusting in crates in their yards for lack of funds and/or experts to complete the installation of the projects.

In spite of all these bottlenecks, though, the government pressed on with new projects in many parts of the country in the 1970s and 1980s. This was the period of excessive petro-dollars in the world money markets and a large number of creditors were ready to offer money and/or machinery on loan to the parastatals, provided there was a Tanzania government guarantee.

Many of these proved to be abortive projects, so that now Tanzania is dotted with unfinished projects and white elephants, the loans for which the Treasury nevertheless has to repay. The origin of the current unsustainable foreign national debt is mainly attributable to these borrowings.

The final phase of the Nyerere era saw our inability to repay our loans and the accumulation of bad national debt, which began in 1980.

Our imports exceeded our exports then by a wide

margin since agricultural production would not recover fast enough from the disruptive impact of the Ujamaa villagisation programme. Most manufacturing parastatals were running at a loss, unable to produce enough for export or even to meet local demand. Others were closing down. Even the diamond mine at Mwadui was operating at very low capacity.

The government's recurrent expenditure was expanding and would not be curbed because of various commitments. Huge subsidies from the Treasury to finance the parastatals meant unsustainable fiscal deficits, runaway inflation and rapid depreciation of the Tanzania shilling.

While the official exchange rate for the shilling was 9.60 to the dollar, in Zurich or even in Nairobi, the market rate was Tsh70 to the dollar.

The adamant refusal of the government to deal with these economic management problems made a bad situation worse and, within a few years, we found ourselves rated as the second-poorest country in the world. We were the 20th poorest country in the world in 1964 immediately after we acceded to membership of the IMF and World Bank.

The scarcity of consumer commodities caused by the failure of the parastatals and our inability to import enough goods because of shortage of foreign exchange, gripped the country. This led to a futile system of rationing, which resulted in corruption and extreme suffering on the part of members of the public, especially low-income earners.

Because of petrol shortages, Sunday driving was banned. This was followed by actual allocation of petrol and one could not buy this fuel without a permit from a government official specifying the amount allowed.

There were long queues of people at parastatal outlets like the Regional Trading Companies with chits permitting them to buy sugar, soap, salt, sembe, rice, cooking oil, matches, toilet paper and practically all other normal household requirements. Clothing was so rare and expensive that some people used empty bags of cement as normal wear.

The shelves of the other privately owned shops were empty and whenever anything was available, its price was very high.

The so-called luxury items were banned and even those who could secure foreign exchange legitimately, like Tanzanians working abroad, were not allowed to import items like television sets or saloon cars.

Because of the scarcity of goods and the ever-rising prices, those with money started to buy whatever was available even if they did not need such goods immediately. If an official travelled to, say, Iringa, he would return to Dar es Salaam with two bags of rice in his official vehicle.

People found themselves buying extra radios or extra furniture, just because money was losing value every day. Similarly, shopkeepers stocked items which they knew would rise in value tremendously in a month's time.

It was at this time that the Economic Crimes and Sabotage Act was passed by parliament.

Under the law, many citizens and non-citizens who appeared to have substantial assets were rounded up and detained. Some of their assets were seized, many of which were never recovered. Few of the assets recovered were serviceable and there have been claims for compensation ever since that time.

Those who were detained were subsequently released after appearing before a tribunal set up for that purpose. But I know a number of honest businessmen who never recovered from that shock of detention, health-wise or business-wise.

This was clearly a measure that dealt with the symptoms of the disease rather than the cause. It was bound to fail as Tanzania transited from the Nyerere to the Ali Hassan Mwinyi regime." - (Edwin Mtei, interviewed by Stanley Kamana, "The Nyerere Era and the Origins of

Tanzania's Current Crippling Debt," in *The East African*, Dar es Salaam, Tanzania, and Nairobi, Kenya, 17 January 2007).

Nyerere stepped down as president in November 1985 after leading the country for 24 years since independence in December 1961. Ali Hassan Mwinyi succeeded him as president of the United Republic. Before then, Mwinyi served as president of Zanzibar and vice president of Tanzania.

After he became president, he started to liberalise the economy and introduce capitalism in the late 1980s.

Socialism and one-party rule were officially abandoned in the early nineties.

Parliament renounced socialism as a state ideology, and one-party rule ended when the wave of democratisation and multi-party politics swept across the continent following the collapse of communism and the end of the Cold War during that period.

Tanzania underwent radical transformation in terms of political direction when the government issued the Arusha Declaration in February 1967 to build a socialist society. The government nationalised companies, banks, plantations and other major means of production and distribution.

In Zanzibar, the Zanzibar revolutionary government which came to power after the Zanzibar revolution of 12 January 1964 nationalised clove plantations and other properties in the same year.

But the nation's most ambitious programme was the establishment of *ujamaa* villages where the people would work together on communal farms. Individual ownership of farms was abolished and the farms were collectivised to establish communal settlements, except in a few parts of the country where the people already lived very close to each other because of the high density of population in those areas.

President Julius Nyerere reported that by mid-1975 more than 9 million people – almost half the nation's entire population – had been moved into more than 6,900 *ujamaa* villages.

And in 1976, the government rounded up thousands of people in Dar es Salaam who were unemployed and sent them to work and live in the countryside. Many of them returned to their home villages.

The repatriation effort was also in pursuit of socialism and rural development, the cornerstone of the nation's economic growth in a predominantly agricultural country and one of the poorest in the world.

Nyerere defended his policy of socialism and explained that familyhood called for sharing, and that it was the basis of the African traditional way of life. *Ujamaa*, which means familyhood, was his African version of socialism and he called it African socialism.

But socialism failed to develop the economy.

After Nyerere stepped down from the presidency, he remained chairman of the ruling party known as Chama Cha Mapinduzi (CCM) – a Swahili name meaning Revolutionary Party – for five years until 1990.

But even after he no longer served as chairman of the ruling party, he remained in control and was the most powerful political figure in the country until his death in October 1999 at the age of 77.

It was he who chose Mwinyi to be his successor; and it was he who chose Benjamin Mkapa to succeed Mwinyi as president of Tanzania and asked a highly popular contender, Jakaya Kikwete, to abandon his quest for the presidency in 1995 in order to provide room for Mkapa.

He said Kikwete was too young to be president at that time and should wait. Kikwete agreed and was elected president in 2005 after Mkapa completed his two five-year terms as president.

It was also Nyerere who in 1973 decided that the nation's capital should be moved from Dar es Salaam to

Dodoma.

Although the official capital is Dodoma, most government offices remain in the former capital, Dar es Salaam, which is the nation's largest city. It's also the commercial capital.

Dodoma officially became the capital of Tanzania in 1996, and a few ministries have been moved there. The parliament was also moved from Dar es Salaam to Dodoma.

Dodoma was chosen as the nation's capital during President Nyerere's tenure because of its central location easily accessible from all parts of the country. It's now the third-largest city in Tanzania.

The second-largest city is Mwanza on the southern shore of Lake Victoria in northern Tanzania.

It's Tanzania's largest port on Lake Victoria. It's also one of the largest ports in East Africa and handles goods for several countries in the region including Tanzania itself, Kenya, Uganda, Rwanda, Burundi, and the Democratic Republic of Congo (DRC).

It's also a historical city. It was in Mwanza where the Pan-African freedom movement of PAFMECA was founded in 1958 under the leadership of Nyerere. It was Nyerere who called the meeting.

PAFMECA was an independence movement which coordinated the independence struggle in the countries of East and Central Africa and PAFMECA was an acronym for Pan-African Freedom Movement for East and Central Africa. As he stated in an interview decades later:

"After the OAU was established in 1963, I allowed PAFMECA to die out. I'm still quietly complaining, because PAFMECA was a movement of people. It was an organization of the liberation movements, and therefore could be a movement of people."

The context in which he made those remarks is

understood clearly when you read excerpts from the interview which are reprinted as an appendix at the end of the book.

And Mwanza will always be remembered for the 1958 historic meeting and as the birthplace of PAFMECA, one of the most important independence movements in the history of Africa which also played a major role in the establishment of the Organisation of African Unity (OAU) in Addis Ababa, Ethiopia, in May 1963.

Mwanza also is the capital of Mwanza Region. The city had a population of about 380,000 in 2008.

It's also one of the major industrial centres in Tanzania. The industries include fishing, meatpacking, textile and soap manufacturing.

Located in a renowned agricultural region, it handles many commodities including maize and cotton. And as a port city on the second-largest freshwater lake in the world, it plays a major role in the commercial fishing industry which has international ties.

Planes come from as far away as Russia to transport tons of fish for consumption in that country and elsewhere.

The region where Mwanza is located is also known throughout East Africa for its large herds of cattle, making it a backbone of the meatpacking industry throughout the Great Lakes region and for the whole country.

The city is also home to the Mwanza Medical Institute of Medical Research, an institution which specialises in tropical diseases.

The other large cities and towns are Mbeya, Arusha, Tanga, Morogoro, Moshi, Tabora, Kigoma, Iringa, Songea, and Bukoba.

The word Dodoma means "It has sunk" in the Gogo language. The Gogo tribe is one of the largest in Tanzania and the capital Dodoma is located in their home district which is also called Dodoma.

The city of Dodoma is also the capital of Dodoma Region. As an urban district, it had a population of about

330,000 in 2008.

Although the government of President Julius Nyerere made plans in 1973 to move the nation's capital to Dodoma, it took many years before the government started moving some of its offices to the new capital. The National Assembly, also known as Parliament, moved to Dodoma in February 1996.

The Gogo are also the main tribe in the city and not just in the district of Dodoma.

The other tribes in Dodoma Region are Warangi, and Wasandawi who are related to the San, the so-called Bushmen of southern Africa.

But there are many people of other tribes in Dodoma Region from different parts of Tanzania especially in the city of Dodoma which has attracted even more people since it became the nation's capital.

The town of Dodoma was founded during the German colonial period when the country was known as *Deutsch Ostafrika* or German East Africa. And it's one of the main stations on the central railway which runs from Dar es Salaam on the east coast to Kigoma, a port on the shore of Lake Tanganyika in western Tanzania.

The central railway was built by the Germans who ruled Tanganyika from the early 1890s until World War I when the British took over the colony after the Germans lost the war. And the town of Dodoma was built during the same period when the railway was being constructed. It also served as a supply station during the construction of the railway.

After the British became the new rulers of Tanganyika, Dodoma became an administrative centre and later the capital of the Central Province. During British rule, the country was divided into seven provinces.

The other provinces, besides the Central Province, were the Coast Province whose capital was Dar es Salaam; Northern Province with Arusha as its capital; Lake Province with Mwanza as its capital; Western Province,

Tabora being the capital; Southern Highlands Province, with Iringa, and later Mbeya, as the capital; and the Southern Province whose capital was Lindi.

After Tanganyika won independence from Britain on 9 December 1961, Dodoma continued to be the capital of the Central Province. In 1963, all the provinces were divided into smaller administrative units and renamed regions. For example, the Southern Highlands Province was split into Mbeya Region and Iringa Region.

Dodoma also is the nation's central meeting point in terms of road network.

A trunk road connects Dodoma with Dar es Salaam on the east coast. And to the west are roads to Kigoma through Tabora, and north to Mwanza on the southern shore of Lake Victoria. This is in addition to the central railway running from east to west which passes through Dodoma. The Great North Road – also known as C to C – from Cape Town in South Africa to Cairo in Egypt also passes through Dodoma.

The city also has two universities: the University of Dodoma which is expected to have 40,000 by 2012, and St. Johns University of Tanzania. Both were opened in September 2007, and the University of Dodoma is going to be the largest in the country.

Tanzania is divided into 26 administrative regions. Twenty-one are on the mainland and five are in the former island nation of Zanzibar. Three are on the larger island of Unguja which is also known as Zanzibar, and two are on Pemba Island which is also an opposition stronghold. Tanzania's main opposition party, the Civic United Front (CUF), has its strongest support on Pemba Island.

And secessionist sentiments are strongest on Pemba Island – more than anywhere else in the former island nation.

Many residents of Pemba want Zanzibar – the former independent nation which includes both Zanzibar Island and Pemba Island – to secede from the union. And there are those who want Pemba to secede and declare independence as a sovereign entity.

Agriculture is the largest sector of the Tanzanian economy. It accounts for more than 40 per cent of the gross domestic product (GDP) and about 85 per cent of the exports. It's also the largest employer. About 80 per cent of the nation's entire labour force is involved in agriculture.

Only 4 per cent of the land is suitable for agriculture. The country has vast expanses of territory which could be cultivated but, in many parts, geographical barriers and other problems including poor and lack of infrastructure, infestation with tsetse flies, and black flies which cause river blindness, make it impossible.

Tanzania has only a small industrial sector producing light consumer goods including import-substitution items. A number of agricultural products are also processed in the country. But there are a lot of minerals. Some of them have been discovered recently. In fact, Tanzania is one of the largest producers of gold in Africa. It has, at different times, ranked second after South Africa, and third after Ghana.

Tanzania also is the only country where Tanzanite, a highly precious mineral, is found. And large deposits of uranium have also been found in the southwestern part of the country east of Lake Nyasa.

The country also is one of the world's leading producers of industrial diamonds. It also has large amounts of nickel, platinum and other minerals.

Large quantities of gas have also been found in Tanzania in recent years. The gas fields in Mtwara Region which borders Mozambique in the south have enough supply to meet the region's demand for 800 years. The gas is also being used to produce electricity for other parts of the country including Dar es Salaam. The rest is used for cooking.

Tanzania also has large reserves of coal and iron in

Mbeya and Iringa regions in the southwest and it will be used to generate electricity to help meet the nation's demand.

Also a rare mineral, coltan, has been found in Mbeya Region in recent years.

It's found in only a few countries in the world including the Democratic Republic of Congo (DRC) and Russia and is used in the development of missile guidance systems and other areas of high technology including the manufacture of computers and cell phones.

In fact, in the sixties, the coltan the United States used in the development if its missiles came from Congo. And its main rival, the Soviet Union, was the only other country which had a large supply of coltan during that period at the height of the Cold War.

There is also speculation that the Tanzania may have large quantities of petroleum, based on exploratory findings in different parts of the country including the areas of Rufiji Delta and other parts of the coastal region. The island of Pemba and other parts in the Indian Ocean have also attracted investors prospecting for oil.

Tanzania also is known worldwide for its national parks and scenic beauty with many geographical wonders. The majestic Kilimanjaro is not only the highest mountain in Africa; it's the highest lone-standing mountain in the world. And its ice-capped peaks – with all the heat and sunshine in the heart of the tropics – is a spectacular sight adding to its magnificent splendour drawing tourists from all over the world every year.

Lake Victoria, which Tanzania shares with Kenya and Uganda but whose largest part – an entire half – is in Tanzania, is the world's second-largest freshwater lake after Lake Superior in North America. And Lake Tanganyika is the world's second deepest lake after Lake Baikal in Russia.

The most famous national park in the world, Serengeti, is in Tanzania. Another world-famous natural reserve is the Ngorongoro Conservation Area known for its yearly migration of wildebeest between Tanzania and Kenya (Masai Mara).

It's estimated that 250,000 wildebeest perish every year in their long migration in search of food during the dry season.

The area is also known for other spectacular views. And it's the area where Dr. L.S.B. Leakey with his wife Mary found what are believed to be the remains of man's earliest ancestor, or one of the earliest. They found the remains in the Olduvai Gorge in the Ngorongoro Crater. And the Olduvai Gorge is generally referred to as the cradle of mankind by many people in the scientific community around the world.

Considering its size, Tanzania is a sparsely populated country. But there are areas of high density, especially in the highlands of the northeast and southwest, along the coast and in the northwestern part of the country, and in the former island nation of Zanzibar.

Most of the black Africans in Tanzania belong to the Bantu linguistic group and speak related languages.

The Sukuma is the largest ethnic group with about 3 million people. They live mostly in Mwanza Region south of Lake Victoria in northern Tanzania.

The other large ethnic groups include the Nyamwezi, the second-largest, who are also closely related to the Sukuma; the Haya, the Chaga, the Nyakyusa, the Gogo, and the Ha, also known as Waha in Kiswahili. Each of these groups has more than 1 million people.

The Hehe, the Yao, the Makonde, the Ngoni, and the Pare are also some of the major ethnic groups in terms of numbers.

And they are all Bantu groups.

Nilotic groups include the Maasai and the Luo.

There are also many Hutus and Tutsis who are citizens of Tanzania. The majority of them were once refugees who later applied for citizenship after fleeing from the turmoil in their home countries of Rwanda and Burundi which have been wracked by civil wars through the years since independence and even before then.

The vast majority of the people in the former island nation of Zanzibar migrated from the mainland through the centuries and even comparatively recently in the twentieth century. For example, Abeid Karume, the first president of Zanzibar after the January 1964 revolution which overthrew the Arab sultanate, was of Malawian origin. Malawi was known as Nyasaland before independence and many Nyasas settled in Zanzibar during and before British colonial rule.

Both the mainland and the isles have significant numbers of racial minorities, mainly Indians and Arabs. Zanzibar has a higher percentage of people of Persian origin who trace their ancestry to Shiraz in what is now Iran which was known as Persia until 1935.

On the mainland, one of the most prominent national leaders is Rostam Aziz, an Iranian – a Tanzanian of Iranian origin – and member of a parliament who has been highly influential in national politics in recent years, including the 2005 presidential election.

People of Asian, Arab, and European origin especially British, have also played and continue to play important roles in national life.

They include Amir H. Jamal, of Indian origin, who was a cabinet member for many years since independence and one of the most prominent Third World leaders; Derek Bryceson, of British origin, who was also in the first independence cabinet like Jamal and continued to be a cabinet minister through the years; Dr. Leader Sterling, also of British origin, and cabinet member under Nyerere; Abdulrahman Mohammed Babu, an Arab from Zanzibar, who was one of the most prominent cabinet members n the union government.

Others include Dr. Salim Ahmed Salim, an Arab from Zanzibar, who once served as Tanzania's permanent

26

representative to the UN for many years and later as prime minister, minister of foreign affairs, and minister of defence at different times under Nyerere.

He was also the longest-serving secretary-general of the Organisation of African Unity (OAU) and reportedly stayed in that post for a long time because of Nyerere's support. When Nyerere stepped down from the presidency in 1985, he asked Salim to run for president but Salim declined, according to Salim himself at a press conference in Dar es Salaam, Tanzania, in 2005 when he was running for president.

But Salim's quest for the presidency also highlighted some fault lines in the nation where divisions on the basis of ethnic and racial identity seem to have acquired some kind of "legitimacy"since the introduction of multi-party politics in the early and mid-nineties.

Some people were resolutely opposed to his candidacy simply because he was an Arab. Salim invoked Nyerere's legacy and commitment to racial equality to condemn his detractors. As one Tanzanian writer, Godfrey Mwakikagile, states in his book *Life in Tanganyika in The Fifties*:

"Europeans may have divided us - in fact only about 171 ethnic groups out more than 1,000 across Africa were split by colonial boundaries - but they also united us. As Nyerere conceded, colonialism created a sense of oneness among Africans.

But it is a oneness that has come under severe strain during the post-colonial era as has been clearly demonstrated by ethnic conflicts in many African countries simply because many people don't accept each other and would rather favour members of their own tribes than treat everybody as an equal.

That was not the case during colonial rule. Tribal or ethnic conflicts as open warfare were rare. It is as if we needed colonial rulers to maintain peace and hold us together.

Once they left, we turned against each on ethnic or tribal basis in an orgy of violence in many cases never witnessed before even in the past.

And large chunks of Africa are still blood-soaked on an unprecedented scale.

Tanzania has been spared this scourge in its most virulent form. But tribalism is a potent force anywhere on the continent especially in sub-Saharan Africa and it is a potential danger that cannot be ignored even in Tanzania. We ignore it only at our peril.

In fact, since the introduction of multiparty democracy in Tanzania in the early nineties, unscrupulous elements have tried to exploit ethnoregional rivalries and loyalties in pursuit of partisan interests to the detriment of national unity.

They include leaders of the Civic United Front (CUF) in Zanzibar, especially on Pemba island; and Reverend Christopher Mtikila, the leader of the Democratic Party on Tanzania mainland who wants the union dissolved and is openly hostile towards Tanzanians of Asian origin, Arabs and other non-blacks and wants them expelled from the country. And there are others of his ilk, with the same warped mind.

Mtikila espouses doctrines reminiscent of the African National Congress (ANC) in Tanganyika in the late fifties and early sixties when the party was led by Zuberi Mtemvu and was virulently anti-white, anti-Asian and against other non-blacks even if they were citizens of Tanganyika. The party's doctrine of Tanganyika for Tanganyikans echoed the sentiments of other racial purists whose invocation of the slogan 'Africa for Africans' meant only one thing: Africa for black Africans.

It was divisive then, and it is divisive today. And so is tribalism which has torn the social fabric of many African countries and continues to do so. It is a continental phenomenon and a perennial problem.

Although Tanzania may have been spared the agony, it is not immune from this deadly disease, this malignant cancer of tribalism and racism, and may one day suffer the same way other African countries have. As Professor Haroub Othman, a Tanzanian originally from Zanzibar who taught at the University of Dar es Salaam, stated in his lecture, "Mwalimu Julius Nyerere: An Intellectual in Power," delivered at the University of Cape Town on 14 October 2005:

'Julius Nyerere was always non-racial in his perspective, and this at times got him into conflict with his colleagues both in the ruling Party and Government.

During the days of the struggle for Tanganyika's independence, he rejected the position of the 'Africanists' within TANU who put forward the slogan 'Africa for Africans,' meaning black Africans.

In 1958 at the TANU National Conference in Tabora when some leaders strongly opposed TANU's participation in the colonially-proposed tripartite elections, where the voter had to vote for three candidates from the lists of Africans, Asians and Europeans, Julius Nyerere stood firm in recommending acceptance of the proposals. This led to the 'Africanists' marching out of TANU and forming the African National Congress.

It is extremely worrying that this racist monster is reappearing now in Tanzania. Some politicians in their quest for power are using the racist card, as manifested both at last May's Chimwaga Congress of the ruling party, CCM, and in the on-going election campaigns.

It is very unfortunate that no stern measures are being taken against this trend, thus giving the impression that the country's leadership is condoning it.'

Tanzania remains an island of stability in a turbulent region. But if racism and tribalism go unchecked, it could end up being one of the deadliest theatres of conflict because of a combination of highly combustible elements in the country including a large number tribes or ethnic groups (126); significant numbers of racial minorities, and disruptive religious forces especially of the fundamentalist kind among both Christians (exemplified by Reverend Christopher Mtikila) and Muslims especially in Zanzibar who want turn the isles and coastal regions of Tanzania into a hotbed of radical Islam or Islamic fundamentalism intolerant of others.

One of the best examples of the malignancy of racism in Tanzania was the virulent campaign against Dr. Salim Ahmed Salim, an Arab, whose presidential ambitions in 2005 were thwarted by black nationalist elements within the ruling party itself (CCM) who questioned his credentials as a national leader simply because he is an Arab; although he is also of Nyamwezi and Manyema descent on his mother's side, an ancestry rooted in two ethnic groups native to western Tanzania and eastern Congo, respectively, with the Manyema also being resident mainly in what is now Kigoma Region.

His most vociferous opponents were fellow Zanzibaris, black delegates from the ruling party, Chama cha Mapinduzi (CCM) - which means the Party of the Revolution or the Revolutionary Party - at the party's convention at Chamwino near Dodoma in central Tanzania where the ruling party's leaders chose their presidential candidate in April 2005.

His enemies also claimed that he was not a Tanzanian because his father was born in Oman. Yet, as Dr. Salim explained, and as many people who know about his family equally stated, both of his parents were born in Zanzibar; so were his grandparents.

It's also interesting that his political enemies never questioned the credentials of Amani Karume, the president of Zanzibar and son of the first president of Zanzibar Abeid Karume, although his mother is an Arab if being Arab or partly Arab - or being white or of Asian origin - is indeed a disqualification in the quest for leadership in Tanzania. Yet Karume's partial Arab identity or ancestry was never a major factor, if it was one at all, in his quest for high office.

Still, the detractors of Dr. Salim raised questions about his credentials as a national leader and as a true patriot, and in spite of the fact that President Nyerere trusted him and even wanted him to be his successor after Mwalimu stepped down from the presidency in 1985.

During the 2005 presidential campaign, Salim himself publicly stated at a press conference in Dar es Salaam that Mwalimu Nyerere asked him to run for president in 1985 in order to succeed him, and again in 1995, but declined to do so for a number of reasons.

One of those reasons, although he did not publicly say so, was that he faced stiff opposition from some black nationalist leaders in Zanzibar who were resolutely opposed to his candidacy in 1985 and in 1995. And they were just as resolute and uncompromising in their opposition to his candidacy in 2005 as were a number of others on the mainland as well.

Dr. Salim also pointed out that there were many Tanzanians who were of mixed ancestry like him, and many others who were just Arab, Asian or of European stock and were entitled to equal treatment just like any other citizens of Tanzania.

He also reminded his detractors that if such discrimination continued, it would destroy Tanzania as Nyerere himself warned not long before Tanganyika won independence and again through the years when he was president.

Nyerere himself appointed Salim Ahmed Salim ambassador to the UN, minister of defence, minister of foreign affairs, and prime minister at different times through the years; something he never would have done if he did not trust him as a capable and credible national leader; if he thought he was an Arab supremacist as some

31

of Salim's enemies claimed, and if he thought he was - together with Abdulrahman Mohammed Babu and other suspects - one of those who masterminded the assassination of Tanzania's first vice president and president of Zanzibar, Abeid Karume, as his detractors also claimed.

In fact, Dr. Salim held the largest number of the highest posts in the government, at different times, more than any other leader in the history of Tanganyika and Tanzania besides Nyerere himself who also once served as prime minister and had the defence and foreign affairs portfolios at other times directly under his control in the president's office.

No other Tanzanian leader had, at different times, served as minister of defence, minister of foreign affairs, deputy prime minister, and prime minister besides Dr. Salim. And he was, besides Foreign Affairs Minister Jakaya Kikwete, the strongest presidential candidate in 2005 (and was said to have the support of the political heavyweights in the ruling party including President Benjamin Mkapa himself) until some people fabricated a story linking him to an Arab supremacist group, accusing him of being a racist. As Ernest Mpingajira stated in his article 'In Bed with the State' published in *Intelligence* 2005:

'In April this year, two very experienced editors, Said Nguba and Mhingo Rweyemamu, committed what amounted to professional impropriety.

They manipulated a picture of former OAU secretary-general, Dr Salim Ahmed Salim, and cast him as a member of an Islamic terrorist group Hizbu.

At the time this happened, Dr Salim was running neck and neck for the Chama Cha Mapinduzi presidential nomination against the eventual victor, Jakaya Kikwete. Dr Salim looked set to win the nomination to vie for the presidency in the October 30 General Election.

Within the CCM ranks, Dr Salim's encroachment on Kikwete's turf was a major threat and his wings had to be clipped at whatever cost.

The offensive picture was fished out of the archives, manipulated and published on page one of *Mwananchi* Kiswahili daily. It portrayed Dr Salim as a racist and an Arab supremacist who masterminded the assassination of Zanzibar's first president, Abeid Amani Karume.

Foremost diplomat

Naturally, Dr Salim protested, but the damage had been done. For the time being, Tanzania's foremost diplomat will never shake off this tag for the rest of his political life.

The two *Mwananchi* editors, Nguba and Rweyemamu, were given their marching orders by their employer but for Dr Salim, the die had been cast; he lost to Kikwete, who is likely to become Tanzania's president in the October polls.'

Race seems to have gained prominence in Tanzanian politics, although not in national life, in a way it never did before, especially under Nyerere who did not condone such bigotry. And it is a threat to national unity.

It is a tragedy that while others, including the developed countries of Europe, talk about the imperative need for unity, we seem to glorify disunity on the basis of race, ethnicity, national origin and other irrelevant criteria.

Race is definitely a factor and a potent force. But tribal loyalty is paramount in African countries most of which are predominantly black.

And as African countries are fractured along ethnoregional lines, we remain weak in a world where the weak are an expendable commodity especially in this era of globalisation while at the same time we complain that we are being dominated by outsiders." - (Godfrey

Mwakikagile, *Life in Tanganyika in The Fifties*, Second Edition, Continental Press, pp. 80 – 85).

Altogether, racial minorities constitute about 1 per cent of Tanzania's population in a nation of about 40 million, according to 2008 estimates.

Therefore there are about 400,000 racial minorities, mostly Asian and Arab, but numbers vary.

In the sixties and seventies, many Tanzanians, mostly of Asian origin, left the country for different reasons including what they considered to be a hostile economic environment because of the country's socialist policies which included nationalisation of private property as stipulated by the government; hostility towards them by some of their fellow countrymen of black African origin; uncertain future in the new dispensation under black majority rule; and better opportunities in other countries especially in the West.

Most of them migrated to Britain. Some of them were British citizens and already had British passports. And today, there are tens of thousands of Tanzanians or people of Tanzanian origin living in Britain. It's the largest community of Tanzanians living overseas.

There are also tens of thousands of Tanzanians of Asian origin living in Tanzania. They include Hindus, Pakistanis, Sikhs, Goans, Parsis as well as a number of others such as Indonesians, Chinese, Malaysians and Japanese.

Arabs also constitute a significant community. And there are about 10,000 whites who are citizens of Tanzania. A Large number of them are British in terms of origin or ancestry.

Also, a significant number of whites from South Africa live in Tanzania. They came after the end of apartheid in South Africa and they are mostly investors or employees of many companies which have invested in Tanzania since the 1990s.

The religious composition of the Tanzanian population is almost evenly distributed. About 35 per cent of Tanzanians are Muslim; more than 30 per cent Christian; and 35 per cent followers of African traditional religions.

The coastal regions are mostly Muslim for historical reasons. That's where the Arabs settled when they migrated to East Africa more than 1,300 years ago. And they are the ones who introduced Islam.

Zanzibar is more than 99 per cent Muslim.

Tanzania also is home to hundreds of thousands of refugees from neighbouring countries, mainly Rwanda, Burundi and the Democratic Republic of Congo. And it has been a haven for refugees for decades since independence and even before then.

In fact, for decades, Tanzania has had the largest number of refugees in Africa and one of the largest in the entire world. During the struggle for independence, tens of thousands of refugees from the Portuguese colony of Mozambique fled to Tanzania. Many others came from Rhodesia (now Zimbabwe), South Africa, Namibia and Angola when those countries were still under white minority rule.

A large number of Somalis have also found sanctuary in Tanzania after their country collapsed in the nineties. And they have easily blended into Tanzanian society because of the large number of Somalis who are citizens of Tanzania. The country has had a significant number of Somalis almost throughout its history because of its geographical location not far from Somalia.

But such proximity has also caused problems for Tanzania.

Many Somalis who have sought refuge in Tanzania are criminals, robbing people including tourists.

A significant number of Ethiopians have also sought refuge in Tanzania. In fact, one tribe of Ethiopian origin, the Iraqw, has been in Tanzania for centuries.

The Iraqw migrated from the highlands of southern

Ethiopia about 2,000 years ago. They speak a Cushitic language. Only a few other people in Tanzania speak Cushitic languages. They include the Mbugu, or Wambugu, who live in the Usambara mountains in northeastern Tanzania.

As recently as 2008, Tanzania was home to more than half-a-million refugees from the neighbouring countries of Rwanda, Burundi and the Democratic Republic of Congo (DRC). And many of them have been offered citizenship through the years.

In fact, throughout its history since independence, Tanzania has provided sanctuary to refugees more than any other African country. And it continues to do so.

And all the people, including the refugees who have lived in Tanzania for quite some time, are bound by a common language, Kiswahili, which is also known as Swahili.

Kiswahili also is the native language of black Africans in Zanzibar and along the coast. Some blacks along the coast of Tanzania mainland also speak indigenous languages but their primary language is Kiswahili.

Many people along the coast are a product of mixed ancestry, Arab and African, and the only language they know is Kiswahili. They are also known as Waswahili as a distinct ethnic and cultural group.

Kiswahili is the most widely spoken African language in Africa in terms of the number of countries where it's spoken. And it's the only African language which is one of the official languages used in the African Union (AU).

It's also the most widely taught African language in the world. It's taught in schools including colleges and universities in different countries and on different continents more than any other African language and is recognised as one of the 10 major languages in the world. It's the world's seventh most spoken language.

It's Tanzania's national language and is also spoken in Kenya, Uganda, Rwanda, Burundi, the Democratic

Republic of Congo, the Comoros, and parts of Somalia especially Mogadishu. And since 1963, Kiswahili has been one of the official languages of Kenya together with English.

There are also significant numbers of people who speak Kiswahili in Mozambique, Malawi, and Zambia; and smaller numbers in Madagascar, Mauritius, and the Seychelles.

There are also people who speak Kiswahili in the countries of southern Africa including Zimbabwe, South Africa, Namibia, Angola, Lesotho and Swaziland.

Many of them lived or were born and brought up in Tanzania during the days of the liberation struggle when they fled from white minority rule and sought refuge in Tanzania. And the active role Tanzania played in supporting the liberation struggle in southern Africa cemented ties, including linguistic ties, between the people of Tanzania and southern Africa.

The origin of Kiswahili was the East African coast in what is now Kenya and Tanzania – including Zanzibar – where Arabs intermingled and intermarried with Africans for centuries.

The vocabulary and grammar of Kiswahili is African. It's mostly a Bantu language. It's structure also is Bantu. But it has incorporated into its vocabulary many words from other languages and is about 25 – 30 per cent Arabic. A few words come from English, Portuguese, and Hindi; and even fewer from German – for example the word *hela* for money.

Words of Portuguese origin include *meza* which means table in Kiswahili. In Portuguese – and Spanish – the word is *mesa*.

But although Tanzanians speak a common language, Kiswahili, members of different ethnic and racial groups also speak their own languages. At least 130 tribal or black African languages are spoken in Tanzania.

Some of the tribes straddle national borders. They

include the Maasai, the Luo and the Kuria who are found on both sides of Kenya and Tanzania; the Makonde, the Yao and the Makua found in Tanzania and Mozambique; the Nyakyusa who straddle the Tanzania-Malawi border; and the Mambwe and the Nyamwanga who live on both sides of the border between Tanzania and Zambia.

Among non-black African languages, English is the most widely spoken and is second only to Kiswahili in usage. Arabic also is widely spoken by the Arabs and a significant number of black African Muslims.

The largest number of people who speak Arabic live in the former island nation of Zanzibar where the language is widely spoken mostly by Arabs but also by a large number of black Africans and Afro-Shirazis. The majority of the Arabs live on Pemba Island which is the second-largest in the former island nation.

Hindi and Gujerati are the main languages spoken by Tanzanians of Asian origin and other residents of Tanzania mostly from the Indian sub-continent who are not Tanzanian citizens.

Portuguese is also spoken in Tanzania by significant numbers of people from Mozambique living in Tanzania. The majority are black Mozambicans. There are also Tanzanians of Mozambican origin who speak Portuguese which is the official language of Mozambique.

They are mostly members of the Makonde, Makua and Yao tribes and they speak Portuguese in addition to their tribal languages and Kiswahili.

German was also once spoken by a significant number of people including black Africans – even long after the Germans lost Tanganyika in World War I – since the country was once a Germany colony. But most of them are dead and only very few are still alive and speak the language. There are also a few descendants of the German settlers who still live in Tanzania.

One of the most well-known German settlements was in the Usambara mountains in northeastern Tanzania.

Most of the members of racial minorities live in towns and cities across the country.

But there are some who live in the rural areas where they own farms and other businesses. And the vast majority of black Africans live in villages in different parts of Tanzania.

Poverty continues to be a major problem in Tanzania especially for the vast majority of the people in the rural areas. The introduction of free-market policies has done little to alleviate their plight.

For people who knew Tanzania or lived in Tanzania in the sixties, seventies and eighties, there are many changes which have taken place in the country.

The changes have taken place in the economic and political arenas.

Tanzania now is capitalist-oriented. It's also a multi-party democracy although the playing field is somewhat tilted against the opposition because of the dominance of the ruling party in the political arena.

But the introduction of multi-party politics has also sparked and fuelled ethnic and regional rivalries as never before. Some parties are regionally entrenched and draw support from some ethnic groups or tribes more than they do from others.

Religious rivalries have also become a factor in some cases unlike in the past. But they are not very pronounced even in those cases.

Tanzania's main opposition party, the Civic United Front (CUF), is supported overwhelmingly by Muslims. A large number of Arabs, mostly in Zanzibar, also support the party because of its ties to Arab countries especially Oman and other Gulf states, adding a racial dimension to national politics.

This has tainted the Civic United Front and a large number of blacks in Zanzibar don't support it because they are afraid that the party wants to restore Arab rule under which they suffered so much for centuries.

The Civic United Front is also handicapped in another respect. It's regionally entrenched. Its biggest support comes from Zanzibar, mainly Pemba Island, and is weak on the mainland.

Other parties have also been compromised by ethno-regional bias.

The United Democratic Party (UDP) is strongest around Lake Victoria – in areas south of the lake – inhabited mostly by the Sukuma, Tanzania's largest ethnic group.

Its current leader, John Cheyo, is a Sukuma himself and comes from that part of the country. He's a member of parliament representing a constituency in that region.

But ethnic sentiments in the 1995 presidential election did not help him to win the presidency. And they couldn't have since the Sukuma don't constitute the majority of the people in Tanzania although they do in their region and threw their weight behind him in his quest for the presidency as they did in parliamentary elections.

Another leader, Augustine Mrema, a member of the Chaga tribe indigenous to Kilimanjaro Region who also was the presidential candidate of the National Council for Construction and Reform (NCCR) party, got overwhelming support from his fellow tribesmen – far more than he did anywhere else – but did not win the presidency because of his limited base.

He once served as a cabinet member and vice premier when he was in the ruling party (CCM) before he left to join the opposition.

Another party, Chadema – Chama Cha Democrasia na Maendeleo (the Party for Democracy and Development or Progress) – is also solidly anchored in northeastern Tanzania where it draws its strongest support from the Chaga and the Pare, the main ethnic groups in that region, although it has tried to expand its national base probably more than any other opposition party in Tanzania and may enhance its stature and status as a truly national party.

Even Nyerere once said in the 1990s that Chadema had the best chance to become a strong opposition party across the country among all the parties in the opposition camp.

The national chairman of Chadema during that time, Edwin Mtei, interpreted the compliment by Nyerere as a cryptic message with hidden meaning. He said it was difficult to know what Nyerere really meant when said that, shrewd as he was.

And one party, the Democratic Party led by the Reverend Christopher Mtikila, is unabashedly Christian in its ideological orientation in a secular state. Yet, it betrays Christian principles by preaching racism. Mtikila has openly attacked Tanzanians of Asian ancestry, denouncing them as exploiters of the black African majority who have no right to live in Tanzania.

Mtikila has not only called for the expulsion of non-black Tanzanians of Arab, Asian and other origins; he has also accused former presidents, Nyerere and Mkapa, of ruining the country because they were not Tanzanians.

He said Nyerere was a Tutsi from Rwanda and Mkapa a Mozambican – a member of the Makonde tribe – and both did not care about the country because they were not citizens and indigenous to Tanzania. He was taken to court by the government for insulting the former presidents.

Mtikila has also called for the dissolution of the Union of Tanganyika and Zanzibar and has vehemently attacked Islam in a country where religious tolerance is cherished as a virtue by people of all faiths.

All those divisions were virtually unheard of when the country was under one-party rule.

This does not necessarily mean that the one-party system was best for the country. But it does mean that multi-party democracy, with all its advantages, has encouraged divisions in the country along racial, tribal and regional lines; it has also encouraged and emboldened many people to openly articulate views which were unacceptable and considered repugnant – and even

41

treasonous – in the past.

Those views are still not accepted today, and many Tanzanians of all races consider them to be anathema. But they have found a platform they did not have before, especially under the leadership of Nyerere whose moral stature was a national asset and played a major role in neutralising such sentiments.

Many changes have also taken place in the economic arena after the introduction of capitalism which replaced socialism.

The economy has improved remarkably. During the socialist era, retarded economic growth was the norm rather than the exception despite achievements in some areas especially in terms of social equality and access to social services for the poor.

Medical service was free, education was also free, and Tanzania had the highest literacy rate, over 90 per cent, in Africa. It also had one of the highest literacy rates in the world – higher than India's, a country which has the largest number of scientists after the United States and the former Soviet Union.

Yet, in spite of all those achievements under Nyerere, the country also suffered under socialism and would have done better economically if it pursued capitalism.

But the introduction, or reintroduction, of capitalism in Tanzania has also opened fissures in society. While a significant number of people have improved their lives economically and some have even been able to accumulate wealth under free-market policies, the vast majority of the people are still mired in poverty and are no better off now than they were under socialism.

In fact, many of them are poorer than they were in the past, prompting some – including university students – to call for a return to the status quo ante and reintroduce the leadership code and other aspects of the Arusha Declaration to curb predatory instincts in society which is dominated by the rich at the expense of the masses.

The biggest beneficiaries of the new free-market policies are members of the upper class and the middle class. The vast majority of the people have been left out, with nothing trickling down to them. They are trapped in a vicious cycle of poverty.

Even some members of parliament including those from the ruling party have warned that the country could be plunged into chaos if nothing is done to alleviate the plight of the poor.

And people see everyday that the rich are getting richer, and the poor are getting poorer. That is a recipe for catastrophe.

While all those are legitimate complaints, there's also no question that social divisions in the country have also assumed a racial character.

Many black Africans blame Tanzanians of Asian origin for their plight. They say they are exploiting them. And some unscrupulous politicians have taken advantage of that and have resorted to highly inflammatory rhetoric to whip up racist sentiments against their fellow countrymen who are not black and whom they say don't belong there. And they're adept at expressing those feelings.

While they have a legitimate case when they say that the majority of Tanzanians are trapped in poverty, they use coded language to promote a racist agenda when they contend that the nation's wealth belongs to the indigenous people, meaning members of black African tribes or ethnic groups.

They have used a Swahili term – *uzawa* – for that, which automatically excludes citizens who are not indigenous to Tanzania, a pointed reference to Tanzanians of Asian origin and others that they are not entitled to the nation's wealth.

The majority of Tanzanians who are black may share those sentiments. But they don't always express them in public. Tanzania's history as a peaceful country has a lot do with that.

Differences among the vast majority of Tanzanians are usually settled through dialogue. With all the problems the people face, there's still a very high degree of tolerance in the country.

Racism and tribalism have never been major problems in Tanzania, although the new economic policies in this era of globalisation have definitely accentuated cleavages and fuelled resentment against some people especially Tanzanians of Asian origin.

There's sometimes resentment even against some indigenous Tanzanians such as the Chaga, the Haya and the Nyakyusa, three tribes or ethnic groups which have produced the largest number of educated people in Tanzania through the decades before and after independence and who occupy a disproportionately large number of positions in government and in the economic and social arena.

But most Tanzanians are not ready to plunge their country into chaos unless pushed to the extreme. And it's unthinkable that what happened in South Africa – where black African immigrants were attacked by black South Africans who accused them of stealing their jobs and even their women – will happen in Tanzania.

Even Kenya exploded after the government of President Mwai Kibaki rigged elections in 2007. About 1,500 people were killed and more than 600,000 left homeless. The violence was perpetrated along ethno-regional lines.

Yet, for many years Kenya was hailed as an anchor of stability in a turbulent region. When the country was about to explode, Kenyans of Asian origin and others fled to Tanzania for their own safety.

And the contrast is glaring.

People in Tanzania don't pick up pangas and machetes hacking their neighbours to death or burning them alive in their huts and churches simply because they're members of other tribes as they did in Kenya.

They don't hunt them down - telling members of other tribes "Get Out! And Go Back where you came from!" - simply because they're not native or indigenous to some districts and regions where they have moved to. That's unthinkable in Tanzania.

Tanzania is the only country in the region which has not been rocked by civil strife of that magnitude.

That is why the country is an island of stability in the region taking in refugees form neighbouring countries.

And it continues to be an anchor of stability and a haven for refugees as it always has been since independence.

Chapter Two:

Towns and Cities

ALTHOUGH most of the people in Tanzania live in the rural parts of the country, urban areas are playing an increasingly important role in national life as hubs of industrial activity, home to institutions of higher learning, and as centres of modernisation including provision of social services not available in the rural areas.

And each part of the country has towns or cities which attract significant numbers of people from the rural areas and other parts of Tanzania; their magnetic power enhanced by a common belief that life in urban centres is easier and better than life in the villages and other rural areas.

We have already looked at Dodoma in the central part of the country. And Dar es Salaam is the subject of a separate chapter.

The former capital is the focus of an entire chapter because of its status as the nation's commercial centre. In fact, more than 70 per cent of all the money spent in Tanzania circulates in Dar es Salaam; a disparity which has a negative impact on the nation's development. Other regions are virtually left. The disparity perpetuates regional imbalance in terms of development and should be redressed.

We are going to look at the other urban centres starting in the southwestern part of the country.

There are two urban centres of significance in Mbeya Region in southwestern Tanzania. One is Mbeya, the capital of Mbeya Region; and the other one is Tukuyu, the capital of Rungwe District.

Mbeya is the fourth-largest city in Tanzania, surpassed by Dar es Salaam, the largest; Mwanza, second-largest, and Dodoma, third-largest.

In 2005, Mbeya had a population of more than 280,000 people.

Mbeya Region also once served as the capital of the Southern Highlands Province during British colonial rule after the provincial capital was moved from Iringa.

After independence in December 1961, the Southern Highlands Province was divided into two regions: Mbeya Region and Iringa Region. That was in 1963. The other provinces were also split up in the same year.

Mbeya Region has more than 2 million people. The largest ethnic group is the Nyakyusa with more than 1 million people.

The home district of the Nyakyusa is Rungwe but as the largest ethnic group in Mbeya, they have spread and settled in other parts of the region.

Mbeya is the largest city in southwestern Tanzania and the gateway to southern Africa.

Mbeya is only a few miles from Zambia and Malawi and is destined to play a major role in Tanzania's economic development because of the country's strong ties

48

to its neighbours and other parts of southern Africa.

It's at an altitude of 5,500 feet in a narrow valley surrounded by high mountains.

Mbeya was founded in the early 1900s during German colonial rule, and one of the most conspicuous symbols of German presence in the town of Mbeya was a German School which later became one of the best schools in colonial Tanganyika during British rule.

The British took over the buildings and premises of the German School and renamed it Mbeya School in 1942.

The development of Mbeya as a town was spurred by the gold rush in the region in 1905, and it became a gold-mining town in the 1920s not long after the British became the new rulers of Tanganyika following the end of World War I in which the Germans lost the colony.

But gold mining did not become a major economic activity around Mbeya. The quest for gold centred mainly in Chunya District north of Mbeya where mining continued for many years, as it still does today although on a much smaller scale. Chunya is one of the administrative districts in Mbeya Region. Its capital is also called Chunya.

Mbeya is fast becoming one of Tanzania's major industrial centres. It also has one of the few referral hospitals in the country.

There are only four referral hospitals in the entire country. The first and most prominent one is Muhimbili National Hospital in Dar es Salaam. It's also part of the Muhimbili University College of Health Sciences and serves eastern regions of Tanzania. It's also the nation's main hospital.

The other three major hospitals in Tanzania are Mbeya Referral Hospital which serves the Southern Highlands comprising four regions; Kilimanjaro Christian Medical Centre in Moshi for regions in northern Tanzania; and Bugando Hospital in Mwanza which serves the west.

The four regions served by Mbeya Referral Hospital

are Mbeya, Iringa, Rukwa, and Ruvuma.

Mbeya is also renowned as an educational centre. It has a number of secondary schools and institutions of higher learning including the highly-rated Mbeya Institute of Science and Technology, formerly known as Mbeya Technical College, offering degrees and diplomas; Tanzania Institute of Accountancy; Mzumbe University, Mbeya campus, a public university offering degrees in social sciences, natural science, and law; Teofilo Kisanji University, offering degrees in education and theology as well as other courses; Uyole Agricultural Research Institute, and other colleges.

The government also has plans to build a variety of industries in Mbeya.

Mbeya has a cool climate, attributed to its location at a high altitude and to the fact that it's an integral part of the Southern Highlands. It also has abundant rainfall.

The area around Mbeya is sometimes referred to as "the Scotland of Africa" but the hills and vegetation are similar to the plants and topography of the Western Cape Province in South Africa – far more than they are to the Highlands of Scotland.

Mbeya also is the main tourist centre of southwestern Tanzania. It 's also a major commercial centre for agricultural commodities from surrounding areas and districts including Rungwe District which is one of the most fertile in the country and in the entire East Africa.

About 40 miles south of Mbeya is the town of Tukuyu. It was founded by the Germans, during German colonial rule, and was named Neu Langenburg. And they are the ones who first made it the district headquarters of Rungwe District.

The town was twice destroyed by earthquakes, in 1910 and 1919, but was rebuilt by the Germans and later by British after they took over Tanganyika. And it's still the headquarters of Rungwe District today.

The National Institute for Medical Research has a

major Medical Research Station in the town of Tukuyu. The town is also a tourist centre and one of the main towns on the road to the neighbouring country of Malawi. It has a population of about 50,000.

Only a few miles north of the town of Tukuyu is Rungwe Mountain, the third-highest in Tanzania after Mount Kilimanjaro and Mount Meru in northeastern Tanzania.

The town gets plenty of rain and Rungwe District gets the highest amount of rainfall in the entire Southern Highlands.

And the district's economic development is inextricably linked with Mbeya which is growing in importance as one of the nation's commercial centres.

The fifth-largest city in Tanzania after Mbeya is Arusha.

It's also known as an international conference centre in Tanzania and East Africa. When major international conferences are not held in Dar es Salaam, they usually take place in Arusha. And a lot of times, the government likes to hold such conferences in Arusha.

Arusha is also the headquarters of the East African Community (EAC). The EAC members are Kenya, Uganda, Tanzania, Rwanda and Burundi. It's also the future capital of the proposed East African Federation, if the five countries ever unite.

It's also served by Kilimanjaro International Airport, one of the largest modern airports in Africa, located between Moshi and Arusha.

Located below Mount Meru, Arusha has a population of about 270,500. It is surrounded by a magnificent scenery and is close to some of the world's most renowned national parks and other sites of natural beauty including Serengenti, Ngorongoro Crater, Olduvai Gorge, Tarangire National Park, Lake Manyara, and Mount Kilimanjaro. It also has its own park, the Arusha National Park.

And because of all that, it's also a major tourist centre

51

in Tanzania, the most prominent besides Dar es Salaam and Zanzibar.

In fact, many tourist trips to different parts of Tanzania start from Arusha. It's a favourite city for tourists and other foreigners; its appeal enhanced by its excellent weather and climate, and strategic location as a regional meeting point.

People have direct access to Arusha from Kenya – also a major tourist destination – and Uganda as well as other countries in the region and beyond.

The town's international status was further enhanced when the UN Security Council in 1994 chose Arusha to be the seat of the International Criminal Tribunal for Rwanda (ICTR) which handled cases of the Rwanda genocide. It officially became a city in July 2006.

It was also in Arusha where *Hatari!* featuring John Wayne was filmed in 1962.

Arusha also has a clock tower which is supposed to be the midpoint between Cape Town and Cairo And the Great North Road from Cape to Cairo – C to C – also passes through Arusha.

And despite its proximity to the equator, Arusha has a cool climate because of its high altitude. And it serves as a major commercial centre for surrounding areas. A large share of the agricultural commodities going through or processed in Arusha goes to Europe. They include flowers and vegetables.

It's also a growing industrial centre. Arusha has a number of factories including a brewery, a tyre plant, and a large pharmaceutical manufacturer.

Tanzania's unique mineral, Tanzanite, is also mined not far from the city of Arusha.

Next we look at Tanga, what was once the second-largest town in Tanzania.

It's now the sixth-largest city in the country and the capital of Tanga Region.

The city had a population of about 244,000 people in

2008.

Its history also is inextricably linked with the history of the country as a whole.

Tanga played a major role in the First World World as a landing site and as a combat theatre in some of the bloodiest battles during the war.

The Battle of Tanga was the first major military engagement that took place in Africa in World War I. Also known as the Battle of the Bees, it was a disastrous amphibious attack on Tanga by the British Indian Army in an attempt to capture German East Africa – what is Tanzania today – in November 1914.

The invading force of about 8,000 Indian soldiers, sent to German East Africa from British India, was routed by the Germans led by the renowned Colonel Paul von Lettow-Vorbeck who won distinction as a military commander in Tanganyika during the war.

The Battle of Tanga was one of von Lettow-Vorbeck's finest achievements, and he was promoted to general for his actions. After the war, he returned to Germany as a hero.

Tanga was then a busy seaport, as it continued to be for decades, and a major entry point into Tanganyika from the Indian Ocean and Kenya which was then known as British East Africa.

Tanga also had, and still has, the oldest secondary school in Tanganyika, known as Tanga School built by the Germans. Today the city also has one of the best known schools in Tanzania and in the entire East Africa, Tanga International School.

Tanga is the most northerly Tanzanian city on the coast of the Indian Ocean. It's also the country's most northerly seaport located about 50 miles from Tanzania's border with Kenya. And it's a major outlet for the nation's export crops and other commodities including coffee, tea, sisal and cotton.

Tanga also is an important railroad terminus

connecting much of the northern part of Tanzania with the coast and the Indian Ocean. It's also linked with the rest of the country by railway and an extensive network of roads and is easily accessible from Tanzania's commercial capital Dar es Salaam.

But in comparison with other cities of comparable size, Tanga is relatively quiet. It also has lost many people through the decades because of economic problems. But it's an important tourist attraction because of its status as a historical city. And some of the country's major tourist sites, including the world-famous Amboni Caves, are located near Tanga.

After Tanga is Morogoro, the seventh-largest city in Tanzania. It has a population of about 207,000 and is the capital of Morogoro Region.

Located at the base of Uluguru Mountains about 120 miles west of Dar es Salaam, Morogoro is a vibrant agricultural centre of a fertile region and one of the nation's centres of learning.

It has some of Tanzania's major academic institutions: Sokoine University of Agriculture, Mzumbe University, and the Muslim University of Morogoro which provides education in various disciplines besides Islamic studies.

It's also one of the main stations on Tanzania's central railway which runs from the coast to the shores of Lake Tanganyika.

Morogoro also is an important tourist centre. Almost all the visitors who climb Uluguru Mountains and visit other parts of the region start their trips from Morogoro. And there are many old German buildings in the city.

Morogoro occupies an important place in the nation's history, including colonial history. In fact, one of the first newspapers to be published in the country was *The Morogoro News* published in the town of Morogoro.

It was published by the British after the Germans lost their colony – German East Africa – in World War 1. But the paper did not last long and disappeared after only five edtions were published.

Although it has an important history, it's Morogoro's status today as one of Tanzania's main urban centres which draws many people to the city. And because of its location in a rich agricultural region, and as one of the country's major railway stations, it's destined to play a major role in the nation's economic development.

The eighth-largest city in Tanzania is Moshi. Located at the foot of Mount Kilimanjaro, it had a population of about 145,000 in 2008 and is one of the nation's most attractive and vibrant urban centres.

It's also the seat of one Tanzania's major hospitals, Kilimanjaro Christian Medical Centre (KCMC), and is known for having some of the best schools in the country, including Moshi International School.

Moshi also is an important tourist centre especially for visitors who want to climb Mount Kilimanjaro.

And there are a number of manufacturing industries in Moshi including breweries.

Moshi also is the capital of Kilimanjaro Region which is renowned for its agricultural products. Major crops include coffee, maize and beans.

And the Kilimanjaro Native Cooperative Union (KNCU) established by Charles Dundas, the British district commissioner of Moshi, in the 1920s was one of the most productive on the entire continent. It was started to help members of the Chaga tribe indigenous to the region to compete with other coffee growers on equal terms on the world market.

Moshi is connected to Arusha on the west by road and is one of the main destinations for travellers from the coast and other parts of the country as well as neighbouring Kenya.

The ninth-largest city in Tanzania is Songea with a population of about 140,000. It's also the capital of Ruvuma Region.

It's named after an African leader who led his people,

members of the indigenous Ngoni tribe, in the Maji Maji war of resistance against the German colonial rulers. The was was fought from 1905 to 1907 and Songea was hanged in 1906.

Many tribes in southern Tanganyika were involved in the uprising and at least 300,000 people died.

As the centre of resistance against the Germans during Maji Maji, Songea District sustained heavy casualties. But today, the city of Songea is destined to play a very important role in the development of the region especially when the harbour of Mtwara on the coast of the Indian Ocean is expanded and becomes a major port handling goods for the entire southern part of Tanzania as well as other parts of the country and for the neighbouring countries of Mozambique, Malawi, Zambia and the Democratic Republic of Congo (DRC).

The tenth-largest city in Tanzania is Kigoma. It had a population of more than 130,000 people in 2008 and is the the nation's major port on Lake Tangayika in the western part of the country.

It's the capital of Kigoma Region and also serves the neighbouring country of Burundi.

And the historic town of Ujiji, famous in the history of European exploration of Africa, is located about 4 miles southeast of Kigoma.

It was in Ujiji where Henry Morton Stanley found Dr. David Livingstone in November 1871.

Ujiji also is the oldest town in western Tanzania and its historical significance somewhat helps Kigoma Region, and the city of Kigoma, maintain a high profile in the country and among travellers from other parts of the world.

As the only major port on the entire Lake Tangayika, Kigoma also serves neighbouring Congo, officially known as the Democratic Republic of Congo (DRC), whose infrastructure collapsed during years of war since the mid-nineties and, before then, under the leadership of President

Mobutu Sese Seko who emptied the national treasury and let the country rot when he was in power for 32 years.

Kigoma is one of the busiest ports on the lake. It's also the only one with a railway connection that works almost all the time, unlike the one in Congo across the lake. There are also ferries carrying goods and passengers on Lake Tanganyika serving four countries – Tanzania, Burundi, Congo and Zambia – all of which share the lake.

Kigoma also connects all these countries to the Indian Ocean via the central railway which was completed in 1915 – the year it reached Kigoma from Dar es Salaam – during German colonial rule when what became Tanganyika was known as *Deutsch Ostafrika* (German East Africa).

The eleventh-largest city in Tanzania is Tabora. It's also one of the most important in historical terms. Founded by the Arabs in 1852, it once served as the capital of German East Africa after the Germans captured it in 1891 and was a major centre of the slave trade conducted by the Arabs.

The town was then known as Weidmannsheil when it served as the centre of administration for the German colony.

It's also home to one of the oldest secondary schools in Tanzania, Tabora School, which has produced a number of Tanzanian leaders including President Julius Nyerere and Vice President Rashidi Kawawa.

Other national leaders, including cabinet members such as Chief Abdallah Said Fundikira who was in the first independence cabinet, also attended Tabora School before going to Makerere University College in Uganda like Nyerere did.

Another prominent African leader who attended Tabora School was Kanyama Chiume from Nyasaland which was renamed Malawi after independence. Chiume grew up in Morogoro, in what was then Tanganyika, and spent most of his adult life in Tanganyika and later

Tanzania.

When Nyasaland won independence, he became minister of foreign affairs under Dr. Hastings Kamuzu Banda, the country's first president, but returned to Tanzania after he and other cabinet members fell out with Banda over policy differences and his dictatorial rule.

Years later, Nyerere said Tabora School was "as close to Eaton as you can get in Africa."

It was an elitist British school where European values were instilled in the students to the detriment of their African heritage. It was also known for its rigorous intellectual discipline.

The city of Tabora also is the capital of Tabora Region, one of Tanzania's largest geographical regions. It's also one of the most productive regions.

Tabora is a major centre of trade and transport, connected by railway with Dar es Salaam on the Indian Ocean, Kigoma on Lake Tanganyika, and Mwanza on Lake Victoria.

Groundnuts, cotton, cattle, tobacco, maize, and other agricultural commodities are shipped from Tabora to other parts of Tanzania and beyond.

In the southeastern corner of Tanzania bordering Mozambique is another important town, Mtwara, on the coast of the Indian Ocean.

It has not attained the status of the other cities we have just looked at – as a major city in the context of Tanzania – but it's potentially one of the most important urban centres in the country.

Mtwara is an important harbour and, because of its strategic location and significance as an outlet to the sea, is destined to play a major role in Tanzania's economic development.

It had a population of about 92,000 people in 2008 and is expected to grow once the area is developed and expanded as an economic zone serving not only Tanzania but other countries in the region.

It's the capital of Mtwara Region, one of the least developed areas of Tanzania, despite its great economic potential which includes natural resources such as gas. Mtwara Region is the biggest supplier of natural gas in Tanzania. The exploitation of gas is also expected to play a major role in transforming the economy of the region, including the town of Mtwara.

Because of its access to the sea and direct connection to the nation's commercial centre Dar es Salaam by sea, land and air, as well as with other parts of the country, Mtwara plays a major role as a gateway into southern Tanzania for a wide range of businesses including tourism. It's a quiet town but vibrant in its own way in terms of providing services to tourists and other people living in or visiting Mtwara.

In recent years, Mtwara has gained special significance because of the Mtwara Development Corridor, a development initiative supported by four countries which are going to benefit directly from this economic development. They are Tanzania itself, Mozambique, Malawi and Zambia.

The corridor runs for about 530 miles from Mtwara on the east coast to Lake Nyasa in the west. And its development will be facilitated by the exploitation of large reserves of coal and other natural resources in the region.

The coal in the region is expected to used in generating electricity vital to development and exploitation of other resources including abundant minerals in Tanzania.

The mining industry is one of the fastest-growing in the country, and the Mtwara Corridor is an integral part of this sector in terms of development.

Tanzania still is an agricultural country and the vast majority of the people still live in the rural areas. But urban centres are playing an increasingly important role in the nation's development. They're also the nation's "melting pot" where people of different cultural and ethnic groups as well as races intermingle, creating a lively mixture and a fusion of cultures.

And because of their magnetic power, they continue to attract large numbers of people from the countryside who believe, erroneously, that life is always better and easier in the towns and cities across the country than it is in the villages.

That was one of the biggest concerns of Nyerere when he was president of Tanzania. He focused on rural development probably more than anywhere else because that is where the majority of Tanzanians live. He also wanted to dispel the myth that national development is centred in towns and cities and that urban areas were the engine of progress for the nation.

Unfortunately, his policy of rural development based on centralisation of the economy through the establishment of *ujamaa* villages proved to be a disastrous failure, good intentions notwithstanding. And it's highly unlikely that he succeeded in convincing many people in the rural areas that life in towns was not necessarily better than life in the villages across the country.

Tanzania's urban centres are growing at a fast pace. Millions of Tanzanians remain convinced that's the only place where they can have better life just like tens of millions of people in Third World countries – including Tanzania – believe that America or Europe is paradise on earth.

They are deluding themselves.

Chapter Three:

Dar es Salaam

DAR ES SALAAM is a city and a region. There is a city called Dar es Salaam, and there is an administrative region called Dar es Salaam, just as there is a city named New York and a state named New York.

Dar es Salaam is the largest city in Tanzania in terms of area and population. And Dar es Salaam Region is the smallest in terms of area.

The city of Dar es salaam constitutes the core of this administrative region and has the largest population in the entire region. In fact, the region itself is formed around the city and it exists because of the city. Without the city of Dar es Salaam, there would be no region called Dar es Salaam.

Our focus in this chapter is on the city of Dar es Salaam, not on the region, and we are going to look at this metropolis from a historical and contemporary perspective to get a comprehensive picture of what is, unquestionably, one of the most important cities or urban centres on the entire continent.

The site where Dar es Salaam was built was known as Mzizima. And many people, some out of nostalgia for a bygone era, still call Dar es Salaam, Mzizima, in honour of a village that once existed there.

There are conflicting interpretations of what the name Dar es Salaam really means.

There are those who say it means "abode of peace." But the most common interpretation which has gained currency through the years is that Dar es Salaam means "haven of peace," not very much different from what's supposed to be the literal or correct meaning in Arabic - "abode of peace."

The original inhabitants of the area were members of the Zaramo tribe. And many of them still live in Dar es Salaam today just as they do in the surrounding areas, although the city itself is not predominantly Zaramo.

It's a metropolis which has drawn people of different tribes from all parts of the country. It's also a mixture of people of different races and nationalities as well as cultures from many parts of the world.

Not only is Dar es Salaam the largest city in Tanzania; it's also the richest.

It's also one of the largest in East Africa and on the entire continent. In 2008, it had a population of more than 3 million people.

It's also the nation's nerve centre in many fundamental respects – from finance to education and much more – and has been the country's economic hub since colonial times when it also served as the capital of the German and later British rulers.

And virtually the entire administrative province of Dar es Salaam, which is officially known as Dar es Salaam Region, is composed of the city whose administrative districts constitute the metropolis. They are Kinondoni in the northern part of the city or the Region of Dar es Salaam; Ilala in the centre, and Temeke in the south.

Since the city itself is the Region of Dar es Salaam, the population of the city is also the region's population.

Officially, the capital of Tanzania is Dodoma. But for all practical purposes, Dar es Salaam remains the nation's capital.

The State House is still in Dar es Salaam, and the president of Tanzania still lives in Dar es Salaam, not in Dodoma, the official capital. Most ministries are still in Dar es Salaam, and all the diplomatic missions are still based in Dar es Salaam.

And most of the national offices of various institutions and businesses are based in Dar es Salaam.

Also, most f the major national and international hotels are based in Dar es Salaam. And all international organisations including offices of the United Nations are based in Dar es Salaam.

Dar es Salaam also is the nation's financial centre. In fact, so much money circulates in Dar es Salaam that the rest of the country plays only a peripheral role in the financial sector.

About 70 per cent of all the money in Tanzania circulates in Dar es Salaam. As one Tanzanian economist, Dr. Daniel Ngowi, explained in July 2008, such concentration of money in one place was not good for the economy and would reinforce and perpetuate the lopsided nature of development among the regions. According to a report in one of Tanzania's leading newspapers, *The Guardian*, Dar es Salaam, 18 July 2008, entitled, "Dar City 'Controls' 70 per cent of Country's Cash":

"An economist has mentioned Dar es Salaam city as the nucleus of the national economy as it controls about 70 percent of all the cash in circulation.

The balance of 30 percent circulates upcountry, a trend

which economists have faulted as not gracious to sustainable and regionally balanced growth of the national economy.

Dr Daniel Ngowi, a research associate at the Economic and Social Research Foundation (ESRF) said recently that concentration of money circulation to the tune of 70 percent for Dar es Salaam only 'was not a healthy sign of the economy.'

While Dar es Salaam controls 70 percent of the national cash, Mwanza, Arusha and Mbeya jointly command 15 percent.

'Unless such a trend is reversed to facilitate, fairly, distribution of money circulation to other regions, the government's efforts to increase incomes of households in rural areas is likely to fail,' he said."

Dar es Salaam plays a major role in determining the rate of economic growth across the nation. And its magnetic pull on the rest of the country is enormous and irresistible.

People flock to Dar es Salaam almost every day from all parts of the country in search of better life.

Almost all the major industries in Tanzania are based in Dar es Salaam. And almost everything new that's brought into the country goes to Dar es Salaam first, making the city an even bigger attraction.

Dar es Salaam began to grow significantly when the German colonial rulers started to build the central railway in the early 1900s from this coastal town. The railway reached Kigoma, a port on Lake Tanganyika in the western part of the country, in 1915.

The completion of the railway ushered in the dawn of a new era for Tanganyika. And the railway went on to play an important role in the growth of Dar es Salaam and other parts of the country through the years.

The coastal town became the most important outlet to the sea in the whole country, and it became the financial and economic centre for Tanganyika, attracting new businesses and industries even though on a relatively small scale when compared with other countries because of the underdeveloped nature of the territory which during German rule was known as *Deutsch Ostafrika*.

During British colonial rule, Dar es Salaam underwent transformation in terms of residential development and demographic composition. A separate area for Europeans was developed and it came to be known as Oyster Bay. And Africans had their own areas, Kariakoo and Ilala.

All those areas – Oyster Bay, Kariakoo and Ilala – were deliberately built some distance from the centre of the town – it wasn't a city then.

The population of Dar es Salaam also included a large number of Indians, as well as Pakistanis but mostly Indians. And they lived mostly in the commercial district of the town where they owned shops and other businesses. They were involved in the retail and export trade. And through the decades, they played a major role in the economic development of the country as they still do today, incurring the wrath of many black Africans who are jealous of them or feel that they have been kept out of business by the nation's Asian population.

After World War II, Dar es Salaam experienced phenomenal growth, relatively speaking, guaranteeing its status as the country's economic hub. And it has remained the centre of economic activity throughout the nation's history even during the worst of times.

It's one of the fastest-growing cities in the world and its population is expected to exceed 5 million by 2020.

The uneven distribution of wealth and income in Dar es Salaam reflects a national trend, and the city itself is, in many respects, a microcosm if Tanzania.

Wealth and high income are concentrated in the hands of only a few people in Dar es Salaam just as most of the wealth in the country is concentrated in Dar es Salaam contrasted with the rest of the regions.

Not only is wealth and income unevenly distributed, a phenomenon typical of most cities in Africa and other parts of the world; industrial development also is unevenly distributed and coincides with racial demographics in terms of ownership and allocation, with most of the high-income-generating businesses and activities being in the hands of Tanzanians of Asian descent and where they live or in areas which they control or where they have economic clout.

Globalisation also has widened the gap between the rich and the poor – and between races since economic status neatly coincides with race, with Tanzanians of Asian origin and others being at the top, and the vast majority of blacks being at the bottom – enabling a significant number of people, including black Africans, to accumulate wealth as never before and in a relatively short period of time; sometimes accentuating cleavages between the rich and the poor regardless of race.

In fact, the disparity in wealth, income and living conditions has become a matter of national concern, with some members of parliament warning that unless something is done to alleviate the plight of the poor who constitute the vast majority of the population, there could be an explosion – social unrest in the towns and cities and other parts of the country; a phenomenon not witnessed before in a country which has a reputation as one of the most peaceful, and most stable, in Africa and in the entire world.

Dar es Salaam has witnessed an economic boom, in relative terms, in this era of globalisation as investors from many parts of the world have flocked to Tanzania to take advantage of the opportunities available in the economic arena, for example, in the mineral sector which has experienced phenomenal grown in recent years following the discovery of an array of minerals.

But little has trickled down to the masses, although even among the poor, there are those who have benefited in terms of new job opportunities in the private sector and even in terms of self-employment which was virtually unheard of during the socialist era except in the subterranean economy, sometimes.

Among the new investors are South Africans who, in this era of globalisation and after the end of apartheid, are now welcome in other parts of Africa to do business; which would have unthinkable in the past because of the country's racist policies which discriminated against blacks and other non-whites; although there has been some resentment among a number of Tanzanians against the new global investors whom they see as predators, exploiting the nation's natural resources and the workers themselves.

But even Tanzania's first president, Julius Nyerere, a staunch socialist until his last days, acknowledged the new realities and just before he died warned Tanzanians against xenophobic tendencies directed especially against the South African investors. As he said in one of his last speeches, "Reflections," which was conversational in nature and tone, at an international conference at the University of Dar es Salaam, Tanzania, on 15 December 1997 about two years before he died:

"South Africa, and I am talking about post-apartheid South Africa. Post-apartheid South Africa has the most developed and the most dynamic private sector on the continent.

It is white, so what?

So forget it is white. It is South African, dynamic, highly developed. If the investors of South Africa begin a new form of trekking, you *have* to accept it.

It will be ridiculous, absolutely ridiculous, for Africans to go out seeking investment from North America, from Japan, from Europe, from Russia, and then, when these investors come from South Africa to invest in your own country, you say, 'a! a! These fellows now want to take

67

over our economy' – this is nonsense.

You can't have it both ways. You want foreign investors or you don't want foreign investors. Now, the most available foreign investors for you are those from South Africa.

And let me tell you, when Europe think in terms of investing, they *might* go to South Africa. When North America think in terms of investing, they *might* go to South Africa.

Even Asia, if they want to invest, the first country they may think of in Africa *may* be South Africa.

So, if *your* South Africa is going to be *your* engine of development, accept the reality, accept the reality.

Don't accept this sovereignty, South Africa will reduce your sovereignty. What sovereignty do you have?

Many of these debt-ridden countries in Africa now have no sovereignty, they've lost it. *Imekwenda* (It's gone). *Iko mikononi mwa IMF na World Bank* (It's in the hands of the IMF and the World Bank). *Unafikiri kuna sovereignty gani?* (What kind of sovereignty do you think there is?).

So, southern Africa has an opportunity, southern Africa, the SADC group, *because* of South Africa.

Because South Africa now is no longer a destabiliser of the region, but a partner in development, southern Africa has a tremendous opportunity.

But you need leadership, because if you get proper leadership there, within the next 10, 15 years, that region is going to be the ASEAN (Association of South-East Asian Nations) of Africa.

And it is possible.

But forget the protection of your sovereignties.

I believe the South Africans will be sensitive enough to know that if they are not careful, there is going to be this resentment of big brother, but that big brother, frankly, is not very big."

Dar es Salaam has been the biggest beneficiaries of the new investment opportunities which have become available in Tanzania in this era of globalisation. And statistics tell the story.

For example, about 75 per cent of Tanzania's industries are located in Dar es Salaam. And about 50 per cent of employment opportunities in the manufacturing sector – in the whole country – are available in Dar es Salaam.

Yet, the city has only about 10 per cent of the nation's population. About 80 per cent of the people in Tanzania live in the rural areas. The remaining 10 per cent are spread out across the nation in the towns and cities besides Dar es Salaam.

Also the consumption of goods and services is highest in Dar es Salaam in terms of percentage. And the best services in many areas of national life, including social amenities, are also available in Dar es Salaam.

Dar es Salaam also is the centre of the nation's transport network. The biggest harbour in the country is in Dar es Salaam. The nation's main railways also originate from or near Dar es Salaam.

Besides the central railway from Dar es Salaam to Kigoma on the shores of Lake Tanganyika in the western part of the country, there is TAZARA, the Tanzania-Zambia Railway, which originates from Dar es Salaam and goes all the way to Zambia and to all the other countries in southern Africa connected by a network of railways and roads which serve this subcontinental region of Africa.

And all the major roads to other parts of the country also start from Dar es Salaam.

The Julius Nyerere International Airport is based in Dar es Salaam. It handles flights to and from all parts of Africa and the rest of the world including Europe, Asia and North America.

Even ships and other sea vessels travelling along the coast of Tanzania and to other parts of the world start their journeys from Dar es Salaam – or end their journeys in Dar es Salaam.

The city is virtually unrivalled across the spectrum, and it has benefited enormously since the 1990s when a large number of investors started flocking to Tanzania after the country renounced socialism and adopted free-market policies.

In fact, the poverty rate in Dar es Salaam is much lower than anywhere else in the country.

And as the nation's hub of economic activities – a trade and industrial centre – the city is destined to benefit from whatever opportunities become available in the economic arena more than any other part of the country.

Not only is Dar es Salaam the nation's commercial centre and still the capital of Tanzania for all practical purposes besides the few offices including the parliament which have been moved to Dodoma; it's also Tanzania's centre of higher education.

Most of the major universities and other academic and research institutions are based in Dar es Salaam. They include the University of Dar es Salaam, the nation's leading academic institution.

It's also the nation's media centre. Most of the newspapers, all television stations, and almost all of the radio stations, are based in Dar es Salaam.

But although Dar es Salaam is also an eclectic blend of different cultures, life styles, nationalities and races from all parts of the world, the people of different races and nationalities don't intermingle as much as they should or could have.

It has nothing to do with racial hostility in most cases. For many people, it has to do with personal preferences, familiarity, different interests and tastes, and cultural differences.

Closest to the city's business district are Tanzanians of Asian and Middle Eastern origin, mostly Indian and Arab. In the suburb of Oyster Bay are many expatriates of all races, especially Europeans who have virtually dominated this part of the city since colonial times when it was almost exclusively for whites, especially the British who were that last colonial rulers.

But Oyster Bay also has a very large number of black Tanzanians and other Africans as well as other non-whites who belong to high-income brackets, although the vast majority of black Tanzanians live in other parts of the city, especially on the fringes of this bustling metropolis.

The outskirts of the city are growing rapidly, populated mostly by black Tanzanians. Many of them are new arrivals from other parts of the country in search of better opportunities in life.

And that will continue to be the case as long as the city continues to be a magnet because of its glitter and glamour as the richest and most developed part of Tanzania.

The urban sprawl that's so much talked about, including its problems which have been witnessed around the world from Brazil to India and from Nigeria to Indonesia, is already here.

Welcome to Dar es Salaam, the haven of peace.

Chapter Four:

Zanzibar

ALTHOUGH the former island nation of Zanzibar is now an integral part of the United Republic of Tanzania, and has in fact been a part of this macro-nation for almost 50 years, it has a very different history.

Its history is different from that of the mainland, what was once the independent nation of Tanganyika, in a number of respects. And it evolved through the years to become a distinct entity with its own character and identity which it still retains today even as a part of the United Republic.

Probably more than anything else, it is its ties to the Arab world which shaped its identity and character through the centuries more than anything else.

Even the name itself, Zanzibar, is of Arab origin. It comes from the Arabic words the Arabs used to describe the East African coast, *zinj el barr*, meaning "land of the blacks."

But there are other interpretations. Some sources say the name "Zanzibar" is probably derived from Farsi, the Persian language, whose word "Zangi-bar" is said to mean "coast of the blacks." And in Arabic, it's "Zanji-bar," meaning the same thing: "coast of blacks."

Whatever the case, it's Arabs who have used the term the most since they were the rulers of the land. And because of their dominance in the region, the name "Zanzibar" probably came from their language: Arabic.

The term "Zanzibar" was used to identify the entire East African coast until the late 1600s. After that, it was used as the name for the archipelago which came to be collectively known as Zanzibar.

And today, more than 90 per cent of the people in Zanzibar are Muslim, adherents of a faith that was brought to the isles by the Arabs centuries ago when they established themselves as the new rulers of this tropical paradise which became famous throughout the world as the spice islands producing cloves, nutmeg, cinnamon, pepper and other spices.

Arabs also still constitute a significant segment of the islands' population and they live in Zanzibar in large numbers more than they do anywhere else in the United Republic.

But they no longer exercise power and influence as they did before, for centuries, when they were the rulers of the islands which they also used as the centre of the slave trade in East Africa.

The slave market was based in the town of Zanzibar on Zanzibar island and it was closed in 1873 long after the slave trade had been abolished in the Western hemisphere, although it continued in that part of the world on a smaller scale even after it was declared illegal.

And when patrols against ships carrying slaves intensified along the coast of West Africa after the slave trade was abolished and declared illegal, slave merchants turned their attention to East Africa, especially to what's now Tanzania and Mozambique, and took some slaves to the Americas as late as the 1820s – 1840s.

It was also during this period that the Arab ruler of Oman, Seyyid Said, transferred the capital of his sultanate from Muscat to Zanzibar in 1840.

Some of the captured Africans from East Africa were taken to South America, especially Brazil. Others were taken to the United States. And some were sold to slave masters in the West Indies.

So, while it's indeed true that most of the slaves taken to the Americas – the United States, South America and the West Indies also known as the Caribbean – came from West Africa and other parts of the continent including Congo and Angola, a number of slaves taken to the New World also came from East Africa, especially from what's now Tanzania and Mozambique.

For example, according to a report in *The New York Times* in 1998, some of the records on the slaves who were taken from East Africa to the American southern state of Louisiana were members of the Makua tribe indigenous to the southern part of Tanzania and the northern part of Mozambique.

The Makua straddle the Tanzanian-Mozambican border. Other tribes in the region also straddling the border include the Makonde and the Yao. And they, together with many other tribes in different parts of Tanzania and Mozambique, also probably had some of their people taken into slavery in the Americas.

In fact, there are documented reports of American ships anchoring in Zanzibar during that period intended to carry slaves, although the diabolical traffic was largely conducted by European merchants in this part of Africa, taking slaves to the Americas; while Arabs took theirs mostly to Arab countries and sold some to Asia.

Although the United States Congress passed a law –

the Slave Trade Act – in January 1808 which clearly stated that importation of slaves into the United States was illegal, the diabolical traffic continued. It ceased only after the Emancipation Proclamation was issued by President Abraham Lincoln in January 1863 and after the southern states were defeated in the American Civil War which ended in 1865.

Before then, as late as the 1830s, 40s and even 50s, Africans were still being taken to the United States in chains, as was clearly demonstrated by the case of the *Amistad* whose captives from the Mende tribe and other ethnic groups in Sierra Leone were set free in the United States after they won their case in court and allowed to return to Africa in the early 1840s.

Although the slave trade was stopped in West Africa especially after the 1840s, it continued in East Africa, and the slave market in Zanzibar was the last one to be closed on the continent.

Yet that was not the end of slavery in the isles. The slave trade continued in Zanzibar and Africans continued to work as slaves and were held in bondage until slavery was abolished in the islands in 1929.

Still, they were not entirely free and remained virtual slaves under the Arabs in the following years.

It was not until the Zanzibar Revolution which took place in January 1964 that Africans were finally free from subjugation and exploitation by the Arabs even if during Arab rule they were no longer held in bondage as they had been in the past.

But their subordinate status under Arab domination amounted to virtual slavery. And oppression by the Arabs played a major role in inspiring Africans to overthrow their masters during the Zanzibar Revolution, one of the most significant events in the history of Africa.

Located between 15 and 20 miles from Tanzania mainland, the former island nation of Zanzibar has many small islands and two large ones: Zanzibar and Pemba.

Zanzibar Island, also known as Unguja, is the biggest and the seat of the capital for the archipelago.

The capital is also known as Zanzibar. It has an old quarter, called Stone Town, which is one of the World Heritage sites. And it was in Stone Town where the slave market was located. After the slave trade was abolished, the market was destroyed and an Anglican Cathedral was built in its place.

Stone Town is the oldest part of the city. It's also known as Mji Mkongwe in Kiswahili which means Old Town.

After the Arabs established themselves in Zanzibar and along the East African coast, they used the islands as an operational base for their ventures into other parts of the continent and elsewhere.

The Arabian peninsula became an integral part of the interaction, mainly trade between the two worlds: Arab and African.

India also came into the picture as trade became a major activity between Zanzibar as well as other parts of East Africa and the Indian subcontinent.

Trade with the East African coastal towns and villages grew gradually, and even became brisk at times, and Arabs as well as Indians established permanent settlements in this region.

It was also on Zanzibar Island, Unguja, where the Arabs built the first mosque in the Southern hemisphere. And they played the biggest role in spreading Islam in East Africa.

Later, the Portuguese gained control of the region and ruled Zanzibar and the East African coast of what is now Tanzania, Kenya and Mozambique for about 200 years before they were ousted by the Arabs from Oman.

The rulers from Oman established plantations on the islands, growing spices, while at the same time carrying on the slave trade. And it was the slaves who worked on the plantations and as servants for Arabs in their homes. The

Arabs also sold ivory obtained from the mainland after killing elephants.

Trading routes used by the Arabs and their African subordinates extended from the East African coast all the way to Congo from where slaves and ivory were taken to be sold along the coast and on Zanzibar island.

The coming of Europeans ushered the dawn of a new era and the Arabs lost. They were supplanted by the new comers and in 1890 Zanzibar became a "British protectorate," just another euphemism for colony.

It was not until 73 years later that the Arabs regained full control of the islands when Zanzibar won independence from Britain on 10 December 1963 as a constitutional monarchy.

But the transfer of power to the Arabs was a clear violation of the fundamental rights of black Africans who were excluded from the government. Had the transition been democratic, they are the ones who would have become the legitimate rulers of Zanzibar since they constituted the vast majority of the population on the islands.

Black Africans were not going to tolerate that and the stage was set for a major change. And it was only a matter of days before that happened.

The change came on 12 January 1964, one month after Zanzibar won independence, and it was a violent one: the Zanzibar Revolution.

The revolution ended Arab domination and brought about fundamental change by transferring power to the black African majority who also had the support of some Arabs and other non-blacks including people of Persian – Iranian – descent known as Shirazis.

Thousands of Arabs were killed during the revolution. A larger number of Indians were also killed. And thousands others were expelled. Many also left the islands voluntarily. And almost all of them were non-black.

One month after the revolution, the new leaders of the

islands established the Republic of Zanzibar and Pemba. And about three months after the uprising, Zanzibar united with Tanganyika to form Tanzania.

Although Zanzibar is an integral part of the United Republic, it enjoys considerable autonomy in the union. The former nation of Tanganyika enjoys none. It does not even exist. It ceased to exist as a political entity when the two countries united in April 1964 to form one country.

Compared with the mainland, Zanzibar is conservative in terms of culture. Its culture has been deeply influenced by Islam for centuries and is deeply rooted in the Islamic tradition.

Zanzibar was also the first region in Africa to introduce colour television. That was in 1973.

By remarkable contrast, it was not until some twenty years later that television service – of any kind – was introduced on Tanzania mainland.

The most vibrant sector of Zanzibar's economy is tourism. In fact, in many cases, the economy is robust only when tourism is in full swing. But it's also possible the islands have oil in commercial quantities whose availability could fuel economic development on an unprecedented scale.

It's an archipelago of magnificent splendour with a rich even if an inglorious past in some cases, especially its involvement in the diabolical traffic in human beings.

Besides its magnificent beauty in terms of its geographical landscape and climate, adorned with luxuriant vegetation in many parts of the archipelago and for which Pemba Island, for example, is well-known, the archipelago's rich past and cultural heritage is written all over the former island nation.

It's a confluence of four tributaries – Africa, the Middle East, Asia and Europe – which has produced an eclectic blend of cultures unequalled anywhere else in Tanzania despite the predominance of Arab influence in many areas of everyday life because of the islands' long

79

association and interaction with the Oman and other Arab nations.

It's also a land of architectural splendour including magnificent doors which lead you into the archipelago's rich past and cultural heritage. They also lead you into the present.

It is, indeed, an exotic place, alluring, yet forbidding in some cases. As one Tanzanian agency, Bon Voyage Travel Centre, describes the former island nation:

"The very name Zanzibar evokes fragrant spices, Sinbad-the-Sailor look-alikes manning dhows with sun-bleached sails across one of the world's most historic water-fronts, sultans with harems of voluptuous women, veiled and clothed from head to ankles in black, and narrow alleys through which explorers marched and slaves were escorted to market.

All that, of course, has changed, though the dhows (mostly small now but otherwise much as they were) still ply the inshore waters and sometimes further.

And though the sultans and their concubines, the slaves, explorers and British administrators have gone, their presence still lingers amid the old royal palaces, along the historic waterfront and among the high, closely-crowded Arab and Indian mansions, markets, shops, bazaars, mosques, cathedrals and one-time slave-markets of Zanzibar Island's Stone Town.

The women clad from head to toe in black still exist, and still wear the Islamic *hijab* (head-scarf) and *bui-bui* (Islamic gown). But few are veiled today and many wear scarves and gowns in colours other than black, often fashionably embroidered, though Islamic modesty and natural grace still prevail.

Men also can often be seen in their traditional Muslim *kofia* (caps) and white *kanzu* (shifts), others wear smart but casual western-style clothes.

The best place to see all this living history, plus some

important Arab and Indian architecture and ornate doors, and to get a real sense of Zanzibar's past - as well as its vibrant present - is in the old Stone Town, most of which would still be recognizable to David Livingstone, Henry Morton Stanley or even Sultan Said the Great. And the best way to see the Stone Town is on foot, with a good guide, all of which we can arrange.

But the Stone Town is only one of Zanzibar Island's many attractions.

There are some beautiful near-white sand beaches, especially on the northern and eastern coasts, and little islands that you can visit by boat, and where you can swim and have lunch, or just relax by the sea.

One island lodge, Chumbe, has won various international awards for its remarkable efforts to conserve Chumbe's marine environment, especially its coral reef, said to be one of the finest of its kind in the world.

Then there is Jozani Forest further south, home of the Zanzibar Red Colobus Monkey, found nowhere else, and perhaps of the rare Zanzibar Leopard, as well as other small mammals and many species of birds. Jozani is a natural forest full of interesting indigenous trees and other plants.

South of Jozani is the little fishing village of Kizimkazi, one of Zanzibar's oldest settlements with a lovely little 12th. century mosque which you can visit. Kizimkazi is also well-known for its dolphins, which you can usually see, or even join for a swim (though don't expect them to hang around waiting to be patted on the head!) just a short boat ride offshore.

Another enjoyable and informative way to pass a morning or afternoon on Unguja (as Zanzibar Island is known locally) is to take a "spice tour" to the island's celebrated spice-growing areas, north-east of Zanzibar Town. This is a "must" for any visitor, for Zanzibar without spices is like a zebras without stripes.

You will be astonished at the variety of aromatic spices

and mouth-watering exotic fruits which you will see growing - and also taste if you take a tour which includes lunch.

Such lunches are cooked outdoors, in an authentic village, by local women, and eaten sitting on the floor (as the sultans did, though they sat on the floor of a palace, not an open-sided thatched hut!) Nevertheless, the lunches are delicious and much recommended.

Spice tours usually incorporate a visit to one or more interesting ruins in the Zanzibari countryside, such as Marahubi Palace or the Persian Baths at Kidichi. Such ruins might be seen in several parts of Zanzibar Island, adding yet another touch of historical romance to this most fascinatingly exotic of islands.

For the more active and adventurous, Zanzibar has some of the best dive sites and snorkeling opportunities on Earth - or more accurately, under the sea.

Excursions and main places of interest on Unguja (Zanzibar Island):

Stone Town and its vicinity

Largely nineteenth century Omani-style town with much Indian influence. Its architecture reflects these influences and various others, while the people you will see in its narrow lanes reflect Zanzibar Town's greater cosmopolitan nature, past and present.

In these streets sultans, slaves, soldiers and sailors once walked, famous Victorian explorers or administrators and veiled women passed each other in the bazaars, the women cloaked in black and in mystery, and perhaps trailing the scent of *oud,* the Arabic perfume.

But the Stone Town is more than a museum. There are good restaurants and hotels, Internet cafes as well as souvenir shops, modern yachts and ships as well as dhows, stores selling electronic goods as well as markets dealing in sharks and swordfish, meat and vegetables and tropical fruits.

And the people in the Stone Town's narrow lanes now include holiday-makers from Italy, Japan, the United States and elsewhere, as well as business-people and locals.

Some of the main places of interest in Stone Town are listed below:

Sultan's Palace Museum

One of several royal palaces, this (and its predecessors on the same site) served as the "town house" of the Busaidi Sultans, looking out across the harbour. Part of a palace complex it was the main official residence within the Stone Town. The museum is furnished in what would have been typical nineteenth century style for members of the royal family. Sultan Said and some of his descendants lie buried in the palace graveyard.

Beit-Al-Ajaib (House of Wonders)

Designed by a marine architect (and looking a little like an upmarket oil rig), the Beit-Al-Ajaib was built as a ceremonial palace by Sultan Barghash. Spacious and airy and with some of the most beautiful carved doors in Zanzibar, it is now also a museum with many interesting exhibits.

Between it and the nearby harbour are public gardens where freshly barbecued lobsters, king prawns, varieties of fish, beef and chicken, eaten with delicious Zanzibari *ajam* (pancake-like bread) or the inevitable chips, can be bought and eaten in the evenings. You can "people watch" while you wait...

Site of Old Slave Market

The main Zanzibar slave market was closed in 1873 and soon afterwards the Cathedral Church of Christ was erected on the site, its altar directly above the place where slaves were once whipped for offending their masters. It is hard to imagine, in this now-peaceful place, the humiliations, and sometimes the horrors, that slaves must have suffered here.

The cathedral exterior has little architectural charm but its interior is inviting and interesting, with various items of historical interest.

Close to the site are the fish, meat and fruit-and-vegetable markets which can also be interesting if you can stomach the smell of fish and butchered meat.

Old Fort

Situated on the seafront, the fort is Portuguese in origin but owes much to later Omani reconstruction. There are craft shops inside and a café. Various exhibitions and shows are held in the fort's amphitheatre.

Livingstone House

Livingstone was invited to stay in this Arab-style house, overlooking the old dhow harbour, by Sultan Majid, while the missionary explorer prepared for what was to be his last expedition into the interior. He never passed through Zanzibar again except as a mummified corpse.

Old British and American Consulates

Situated by the sea in Shangani and once the temporary homes for various explorers (Stanley stayed at the American Consulate, now part of the Tembo Hotel). Livingstone's body once rested in a room, now an office, in the old British Consulate.

Tippu Tip's House

Also in Shangani, this old Arab-style mansion was the home of one of the best-known, most-feared Swahili slave-traders, a man who was often ruthless but also an adventurous and courageous traveller.

Henry Morton Stanley among others had a grudging respect for Tippu Tip, and Livingstone himself was often supported by the very slave traders whose practices he loathed. The house itself is in poor shape but has a fine "Zanzibar" doorway.

John Sinclair's Architecture

Several buildings in Stone Town were designed by the British architect John Sinclair, who was enamoured of the Islamic style. Among his buildings are the State House, the High Courts, the Amani Peace Museum, the Old Post Office and the Bharmal Building.

Marahubi Palace

Ruins of Sultan Barghash's harem, just north of Stone Town. Barghash died before he could enjoy the delights of this harem and in any case it burned down soon afterwards.

It must have been a most pleasant place by the sea, in attractive grounds shaded by mangoes and palms.

Little is left but some old stone columns and a lily-covered pool where the women would perhaps have bathed, but there is a nostalgic, romantic and gently rural air about the place.

Mbweni Ruins

These ruins are in the grounds of the very pleasant Protea Mbweni Ruins Hotel, a little way south of Stone Town. They include the ruins of an old nineteenth century private Arab house, which was bought, transformed and extended to create a school for freed slave girls. Around them is a beautiful botanic garden.

Chumbe Island

Small island a short boat ride from Mbweni Ruins Hotel, lovely secluded place to spend a night or two.

There is an old lighthouse on Chumbe but its main attraction nowadays is its award-winning lodge and the superb coral shelves which provide excellent snorkeling. Glass-bottomed boat also available for coral reef viewing. Rare and very large coconut crabs can be seen on the island.

Changu Island

A short boat ride from the Zanzibar waterfront, this small, wooded island was formerly known as Prison Island, though the prison, now in ruins, was never used. Pleasant little beach and nearby café. There are giant tortoises on Changu, brought from Aldabra, and in the woods tiny suni antelopes and several species of birds.

Beyond Stone Town

Places of interest in Unguja outside the town include Mangapwani Beach and Caves, a pleasant area north of

Stone Town; Mtoni Palace, once the out-of-town home of Sultan Said but now in ruins; Dunga Palace; small ruined home of a local sheikh; Jozani Forest and Kizimkazi (both described in main Zanzibar introduction), and of course a huge number of wonderful beaches, mainly along the 'Sunrise Coast' in the east."

Zanzibar is one of the biggest tourist destinations in Tanzania and on the entire continent.

It's also one of Tanzania's, and Africa's, most fascinating parts in terms of history.

Chapter Five:

The People of Tanzania and Their Ethnic Identities

TANZANIA has one of the largest numbers of ethnic and racial groups in Africa. It also has one of the largest populations on the continent.

It has about 130 ethnic groups indigenous to Africa and is surpassed only by Nigeria which has about 250, the Democratic Republic of Congo (DRC) with about 200, and Cameroon with about 150.

We are going to look at each of those groups to get a demographic picture of the largest country in East Africa, a region comprising Kenya, Uganda, Tanzania, Rwanda and Burundi. All these countries also constitute an economic bloc known as the East African Community (EAC) which one day may be transformed into a political federation under one government.

Each of Tanzania's ethnic groups differs from other groups in terms of culture, language and social organisation, although there are some similarities among a number of groups which share customs and traditions in varying degrees.

The languages of some of these groups are also very closely related in terms of vocabulary and structure because of their common origin, shared history and interactions – including intermarriage – through the centuries.

In fact, some of Tanzania's largest ethnic groups, the Sukuma and the Nyamwezi are very closely related.

But even within the groups themselves, at least some of them, there are some differences in terms of language and culture.

And in most cases, the demographic pattern of the country coincides with geography. Each region is identified with specific groups.

Therefore geography reflects ethnic identities as much as it does in other parts of Africa. For example, Songea District in Ruvuma Region in southern Tanzania is inhabited mostly by the Ngoni.

Bukoba District in northwestern Tanzania is inhabited mostly by the Haya; Iringa in the Southern Highlands by the Hehe, Moshi in Kilimanjaro Region by the Chaga, Dodoma in central Tanzania by the Gogo, Rungwe District in the Southern Highlands by the Nyakyusa, Tabora in western Tanzania by the Nyamwezi and so on, although there are smaller numbers of other people, as well, in all those areas.

Some of the minority groups are indigenous to those districts; for example, the Kisi who live around Lake Nyasa in Rungwe District, while others are not. And some of them are closely related. The Ndali, for example, of Ileje and Rungwe districts, are closely related to the Nyakyusa and their languages are mutually intelligible. They even use the same tribal names in many cases.

Even before Europeans came, different tribes lived in their own areas. The colonial rulers only reinforced these separate ethnic and geographical identities by drawing administrative lines on that basis to create districts which were inherited at independence and which exist unto this day as the basis of administration in post-colonial Tanzania and other parts of Africa.

Although Tanzania has one of the largest numbers of ethnic groups in Africa – for example, neighboring Kenya has only 42 contrasted with Tanzania's 130 – the country has not been affected by ethnic conflicts which have ravaged many other parts of the continent.

In fact, Tanzania is the only country in East Africa which has been spared this agony. And for decades since independence, it has been one of the most peaceful, and most stable, countries on the entire continent.

One of the main reasons for that is the size of the ethnic groups – or tribes – in the country. Most of the groups in Tanzania are relatively small. Therefore there are no dominant groups which have been able to flex muscles and dominate others.

The Sukuma, the largest, has about 3 million people. But that's in a country of about 40 million. And they have not even attempted to dominate the country because of the good relations which already exist among the nation's different tribes whose members are also united by a common language, Kiswahili, and by a strong sense of national identity transcending tribal – as well as regional – loyalties.

But there are tensions between Tanzanians of Asian origin, mostly Indians, and black Africans mainly because of the dominance of the Tanzanian Asian community in commerce.

The hostility towards them is not purely economic in terms of motivation. Racism is also a factor. But it's mostly economic. And the vast majority of black Tanzanians and their fellow countrymen of Asian origin get along just fine. Also, most Tanzanians prefer dialogue to violence in resolving their differences.

The two largest black African ethnic groups, the Sukuma and the Nyamwezi, are not only closely related linguistically; they are also related culturally. And they share a lot of similarities in terms of social organisation, how they live and how they earn their living.

The Sukuma also own large herds of cattle but they are also farmers like the Nyamwezi and other Bantu groups in Tanzania and elsewhere on the continent.

Their traditional homeland is a region south of Lake Victoria in northern Tanzania, and the name of their ethnic group, "Sukuma," means "north" and, in this context, means "people of the north."

The people call themselves Basukuma, which is plural form. In singular form, a Sukuma is Musukuma. This linguistic designation is applicable to all ethnic and racial groups.

The same prefix or something similar to that is found in other Bantu languages. For example, in Nyakyusa language, spoken by members of the Nyakyusa ethnic group which is one of the largest in Tanzania, the people call themselves Banyakyusa just as the Sukuma call themselves Basukuma, and the Nyamwezi – Banyamwezi, and so on.

In Swahili or Kiswahili, the plural is Wasukuma. The singular form is Msukuma. The prefixes Wa- and M- are used to identify other tribes and races in the same way.

Although historically the Sukuma and the Nyamwezi were farmers and cattle owners, many of them now concentrate on agriculture to earn a living.

They are engaged mostly in subsistence farming. But they also grow cash crops and sell whatever surplus they have from the crops they grow for their own consumption. The Sukuma also grow cotton. And the Nyamwezi are also known to be excellent bee keepers.

During German colonial rule, the Sukuma and the

Nyamwezi worked as porters and acted as middlemen in the trade with the Swahili people and the Arabs along the coast. The Nyamwezi also played a big role in the slave trade working with the Arabs.

Besides the Sukuma and the Nyamwezi, another ethnic group which is one of the most well-known in Tanzania is the Chaga.

There's some dispute on how their name is spelt. Some spell it as Chagga and others spell it as Chaga, the former being an anglicized version common even in a few other African names which some people spell with double letters instead of a single letter common in African languages. Even some Swahili people spell their names that way; for example, instead of Ali, some spell their name as Ally.

Whatever the case, the Chaga or Chagga is one of the most well-known ethnic groups not only in Tanzania but in the entire East Africa. And its people were among the first to get education provided by Europeans in the country.

They were also among the first to grow coffee, their main cash crop. And like the Nyakyusa and the Haya, the Chaga are some of the biggest growers of bananas in the country. The Nyakyusa and the Haya also produce coffee in large quantities.

Although the Chaga are indigenous to the area around Mount Kilimanjaro, they also live in other parts of Tanzania just like members of other tribes do. And they are some of the most successful people in business.

The Makonde of southern Tanzania are some of the most well-known people not only in Tanzania but also among tourists from all parts of the world because of their highly valued wood carvings. Their works of art are known worldwide as Makonde carvings.

They straddle the border with Mozambique and virtually form a cultural and linguistic bridge between Tanzania and northern Mozambique, which is also their traditional homeland. And they are some of the most tradition-bound people in Africa, immensely proud of their culture and way of life.

The Makonde are also one of the largest ethnic groups in Tanzania. And because they have lived in virtual isolation for a long time, they have not been very much influenced by modernisation, thus reinforcing their ethnic and cultural identity.

They have had interactions with Muslim traders for centuries. But they have not been influenced by Islam or Islamic culture in a way they normally would have been because of this long interaction had they not been highly defensive of their identity as a people and their traditional way of life. Many of them continue to follow their traditional religion and live the same way they have lived for centuries.

A sample of Tanzania's demographic profile must include the Swahili for a balanced picture because of their dual heritage, African and Arab, among other things.

The Swahili live mostly along the coast and are a product of intermarriage between Africans and Arabs. But members of other black African groups along the coast such as the Zaramo around Dar es Salaam and others are also considered and consider themselves to be Swahili because of the Swahili culture they have adopted and the strong Islamic and Arab influence which has shaped their lives for centuries.

Most of them also speak Kiswahili as their first language, a distinction that also qualifies them to be Swahili or Waswahili.

As coastal people, the Swahili also have a reputation as excellent fishermen and sailors. And their dhows have been used for trade on the Indian Ocean for centuries, trading with Arabs, Indians and other people from Asia including Chinese and Indonesians.

And in many ways, their culture is an eclectic mixture, and blend, of African and Arab influences and to a smaller degree includes Indian elements as well.

In the former island nation of Zanzibar, there are a number of African groups although fewer than those on the mainland. And they originally came from the mainland themselves. Also, almost one-third of all Zanzibaris came from the mainland in recent times. The rest settled in Zanzibar centuries ago.

The indigenous Zanzibaris who include the Hadimu and Tumbatu on the island of Zanzibar which is also known as Unguja, and the Pemba on Pemba Island, and all of whom are Bantu, also include people of Persian or Iranian descent.

The Persians who first settled in Zanzibar in the 900s A.D. were gradually absorbed by the indigenous groups through the centuries, producing a distinct group known as Afro-Shirazi.

But the black African groups in Zanzibar have remained largely intact, maintaining their identities for hundreds of years as they still do today.

In fact, even many of the Zanzibaris who identify themselves as Shirazi, and nothing else, are as black as any other black Zanzibaris. That *is* because they *are* black in most cases, more than anything else, despite their claims to Persian ancestry. Many of them have none, and some of them have very little of it. They're just ashamed of their black African ancestry.

Many Zanzibaris are also descendants of slaves from the mainland including Congo, and Malawi which was once known as Nyasaland during British colonial rule. There are also groups of Comorians, Somalis and a large number of Arabs who once ruled the former island nation for centuries. There is also a significant number of people of Asian descent, mostly from India.

Among Arabs, a significant number of immigrants from Oman settled in Zanzibar in the past several decades. They were mostly poor and are known as Wamanga in Kiswahili. And those from Yemen are known as

Washihiri.

There's no question that the ethnic and racial mixture of Zanzibaris is unequalled anywhere else in Tanzania except along the coast. And it has produced a population that is unique on the continent in many respects. As one Tanzanian journalist, Jenerali Ulimwengu, stated in his article – which was a review of a book by Professor Issa Shivji of the University of Dar es salaam who is a Tanzanian of Indian descent – published in *The East African*, 30 June 2008, and entitled "Nyerere: How He Manipulated Zanzibar":

"When anti-colonial forces in Africa were agitating for independence, different ethnic, racial and class formations vied with each other for political ascendancy.

Zanzibar in particular was a melting pot where groups of varied origins had created a culture, civilisation and language that were distinctly Zanzibari in particular and Swahili in general, belonging to the larger religious and cultural ensemble of coastal city-states that dotted the East African coast from Lamu and Mombasa to Sofala in present-day Mozambique.

The rich tapestry of Zanzibari society brought together not only people from the African mainland, from as far away as Nyasaland (present day Malawi) and Belgian Congo, but also from Oman, Yemen, the Comoros, India and Shiraz in Persia, - who interacted extensively in the fields of commerce, agriculture and the crafts and who, though the idyllic characterisation of social relations on the islands of Unguja and Pemba may have been exaggerated, could not strictly be pigeonholed into the racial hierarchy obtaining on the mainland (Europeans at the top, Asians in the middle, and Africans at the bottom). A unique Zanzibari identity thus came to be a reality, whatever the origins of those who claimed it.

It was the politicians, in jostling for space in the public consciousness, who ushered in the politicisation of race

96

and ethnicity, especially as Independence approached and the prospects of acquiring power beckoned. Thus were born the easy categorisations that sought to place the various ethnic and racial groups into the neat little boxes - Arabs, Indians, mainlanders, etc - that have coloured the politics of the islands to this day.

Whereas Karume and the Afro-Shirazi Party (ASP) accused the Zanzibar Nationalist Party (ZNP) of being Arab feudalists acting at the behest of their masters in Oman, the ZNP suspected Karume and the ASP of being Trojan horses for the mainland (Tanganyika). The bad blood created in that epoch poisons Zanzibari politics to this day."

On the mainland itself, the stunning diversity of its population reflects a neatly textured rich tapestry of multiple identities weaved into one transcending ethnic and regional loyalties.

The groups that constitute Tanzania mainland range from the Alagwa to the Zyoba.

Some of them even look different from each other. But they still see themselves as one people.

The Alagwa are one of the smallest ethnic groups in Tanzania and on the entire continent. There were about 30,000 Alagwa in 2008 and they live in Kondoa District in Dodoma Region in central Tanzania.

They are also known as Chasi and they have their own ethnic, cultural and linguistic identity which distinguishes them from other groups.

And as one of the smallest ethnic groups, they may face extinction which could also be facilitated by intermarriage with members of other groups. But they have, for a long time, shown enough resilience and determination to survive as a distinct ethnic entity.

The Akiek are another small ethnic group in Tanzania. And they straddle the Tanzanian-Kenyan border. They live in the southern part of Arusha Region in northern

Tanzania and in southern Kenya.

There are about 37,000 of them but not all of them speak the Akiek language.

It's a Southern Nilotic language of the Kalenjin group. The Kalenjins live in the Rift Valley in Kenya.

The Akiek of Tanzania are a subgroup of the Okiek, also known as Ogiek. The Ogiek live in both Kenya and Tanzania. They are hunter-gatherers.

Most of the Ogiek have been absorbed by other cultural groups around them and hardly speak their own language. The Akiek in northern Tanzania now speak Maasai, and those in Kenya speak Kikuyu which is also known as Gikuyu among the Kikuyu people themselves.

But they are also bilingual and speak both Maasai and Akiek.

The Arusha live in Arusha Region in northern Tanzania. They are a distinct group but are related to the Maasai.

The Assa are one of the smallest ethnic and linguistic groups in Tanzania. It's estimated that there are about only 350 of them left after their brethren, the eastern Assa, were absorbed by the Maasai. They live on the Maasai Steppe in northern Tanzania

Their Assa language is Cushitic but it's often wrongly identified as Dorobo, a derogatory term used to collectively identify ethnic groups of hunter-gatherers in Kenya and Tanzania who are despised by many people of other groups.

The Barabaig live in the northern volcanic highlands near Mount Hanang in north-central Tanzania and are a subgroup of the Datoga ethnic group. And they speak the Datoga language. But they are identified as a distinct ethnic and linguistic group with their own identity.

The Datoga – collectively a number of subgroups of this larger group – live in the same area and have a total population of about 88,000.

The Bembe live in western Tanzania. They are also

indigenous to the Democratic Republic of Congo (DRC). They live in the eastern part of Congo close to Lake Tanganyika. And just across the lake are their kith-and-kin in Tanzania with whom they interact regularly.

There are more than 250,000 Bembes in the Democratic Republic of Congo, and a large number of them in Tanzania as well.

The Bena live in Njombe District in Iringa Region in the Southern Highlands and are one of Tanzania's largest ethnic groups. Their population was about 700,000 in 2008. And their home district in renowned in Tanzania for the production of wheat, among other crops.

Another group close to the homeland of the Bena are the Nena in the northeastern part of the Livingstone Mountains in the Southern Highlands.

Scottish explorer Joseph Thomson stumbled upon them in 1879 – as he did upon the Nyakyusa in 1876 and other groups in the Southern Highlands around the same time – and noticed they were a distinct group with their own physical features and language. And eighteen years later in 1897, a German priest came into contact with the same group.

But for some inexplicable reason, they disappeared from the radar and nothing was written about them in the ethnographic records compiled by the German and British colonial rulers.

However, in the 1970s, people called Nena were reported to be living much further south in the Livingstone Mountains and are believed to be related to the people who were encountered earlier by the Scottish explorer Thomson and the German priest who went to the same area almost 20 years after Thomson did.

The Bende live in Mpanda District in Rukwa Region in southwestern Tanzania and number about 30,000. They are one of the smallest ethnic and linguistic groups in the country. But they are no credible reports that they face extinction in spite of their relatively small size.

The Bondei are indigenous to the Usambara Mountains in Tanga Region in northeastern Tanzania and had a population of about 90,000 in 2008.

They're one of the most well-known tribes in Tanzania, and their language, which is known as Kibodei in Kiswahili, is similar to Shambala – spoken by the Sambaa whose language is also known as Kisambaa – and to Zigula spoken by the Zigua whose language is also called Kizigua. And like the Bondei, the Sambaa and the Zigua live in Tanga Region.

The Bondei language is also related to Kingulu which is spoken by members of the Ngulu tribe whose population is estimated to about 135,000.

The Ngulu live in east-central Tanzania. They are found in Morogoro District in Morogoro Region, Handeni District in Tanga Region, as well as Mpwapwa and Kongwa districts in Dodoma Region in central Tanzania.

But they are different from the Ngulu of Mozambique and Malawi just as the Kisi in Rungwe District in Mbeya Region in the Southern Highlands of Tanzania are different from the Kisii of Kenya and the Kissi of Liberia, Guinea and Sierra Leone in West Africa – in spite of the similarities in their names.

The Bungu live in Chunya District in Mbeya Region in the Southern Highlands and are one of Tanzania's smallest ethnic and linguistic groups. They are estimated to be around 40,000.

The Burunge are indigenous to Kondoa District in Dodoma Region in central Tanzania. They may be in danger of being "wiped out" through assimilation since there are only a few of them. In 2008, their population was estimated to be about 15,000.

The Dhaiso live in Muheza District at the foot of the Usambara Mountains in Tanga Region in northeastern Tanzania.

One of the smallest groups in Tanzania, they numbered only 5,000 in 2000 and it's highly unlikely that their population has grown considerably since then.

In a way, it's a "dying" tribe because of its very small number. Even Dhaiso children are not learning their native language; it's not seriously taught by their parents and other adults.

The Dhaiso are related to the Segeju, another small tribe with a population of about 15,000 in 2008.

The Segeju also live in Tanga Region between the city of Tanga and Tanzania's border with Kenya. Their language also faces extinction. Only about 7,000 – out of a population of 15,000 – speak Kisegeju, the Segeju language.

The Digo is another ethnic and linguistic group in Tanga Region. They also live in Kenya and occupy a stretch of land on the coast of the Indian Ocean which extends from Mombasa in Kenya to Tanga in northeastern Tanzania.

There are about 310,000 Digos in Kenya and Tanzania. The majority live in Kenya. There are about 90,000 of them in Tanzania. They call their language Chidigo. In Kiswahili, it's known as Kidigo.

They are part of the greater Mijikenda ethnic group comprising nine tribes including the Duruma and Giriama which are Kenyan tribes. Mijikenda means "nine towns" in Kiswahili.

The Doe (the "e" is pronounced as "a" in "angle," a rough approximation) live in Bagamoyo District on the coast in Pwani Region. In fact, "Pwani" means "coast" in Kiswahili. Therefore Pwani Region means Coast Region.

The Doe are also one of Tanzania's smallest ethnic and linguistic groups and had a population of only about 28,000 people in 2008.

The Fipa, or Wafipa, live in Sumbawanga and Nkansi districts in Rukwa Region in southwestern Tanzania. Their population is estimated to be more than 200,000 and are one of Tanzania's larger ethnic and linguistic groups.

The Gogo are one of the largest ethnic groups in

Tanzania with a population of more than 1.3 million. They live in Dodoma Region in central Tanzania.

Historically, they have been predominantly pastoralist, and patrilineal – tracing descent and inheritance through the male line, but many Gogos in contemporary times are farmers. They also live in towns and cities in different parts of Tanzania. Many of them also work on farms, including plantations, in different parts of the country.

The Gorowa also live in central Tanzania. There are about 55,000 of them.

The Gweno are one of the smallest ethnic and linguistic groups in Tanzania with a population of only about 2,000. They live in the northernmost part of the Pare Mountains in Kilimanjaro Region in northeastern Tanzania. And because their population is very small, it's highly probable that they won't be around anymore after a few decades.

The Ha, known as Waha in Kiswahili, are one of the largest ethnic and linguistic groups in Tanzania. There are about 1 million of them and they live in Kigoma Region in western Tanzania.

The Hadza, or Hadzapi, are an endangered part of mankind. They're virtually extinct. There are fewer than 1,000 Hadzapis and are facing pressure from external forces threatening their existence.

They live around Lake Eyasi in the central Rift Valley and in areas near the Serengeti plateau in northern Tanzania and are hunter-gatherers. They have lived the same way for thousands f years and are believed to be the last functioning hunter-gatherers in Africa. They are also believed to be among the original inhabitants of the region.

They are a distinct group in central Tanzania and in the entire country. They are not closely related to any other people in Tanzania.

They are generally considered to be related to the Khoi of southern Africa but modern genetic research suggests that they may be closely related to the Pygmies.

Their language also has click sounds, a linguistic feature which has been cited as evidence that they are related to the Khoi of southern Africa who also use clicks in their language.

The Hangaza, or Wahangaza as they are known in Kiswahili, are one of the larger ethnic and linguistic groups in Tanzania.

They call themselves Bahangaza and are known by that name in other Bantu languages except in Kiswahili (Wahangaza), and in some languages such as Kinyakyusa – spoken by the Nyakyusa of southwestern Tanzania – which don't have the letter "z." In Kinyakyusa or Nyakyusa language, they are called "Bahangasa."

They live in Kagera Region in northwestern Tanzania and are estimated to be about 155,000. Kagera Region borders Uganda.

The Haya are one of the largest ethnic and linguistic groups in Tanzania and in the entire East Africa. There are more than 1.2 million Hayas and they live in Bukoba, Muleba and Karagwe districts in Kagera Region in northwestern Tanzania

The Hehe are one of the largest groups in Tanzania. They live in Iringa Region in the Southern Highlands. There are about a million of them.

They have a reputation as fierce fighters and played a legendary role in the war against the Germans, resisting colonial aggression.

The Ikizu live in Mara Region in northern Tanzania and are estimated to be about 30,000.

The Ikoma also live in Mara Region. One of the smallest groups in Tanzania with a population of only about 15,000, they may be an endangered tribe and could be extinct several decades from now if they don't multiply and maintain their population base.

The Iraqw are unique in Tanzania. They migrated from southern Ethiopia about 2,000 years ago and live in Arusha Region and Manyara Region in north-central

103

Tanzania above the Rift Valley wall and south of the Ngorongoro Crater.

They are concentrated in the Mbulu Highlands in Mbulu District and in areas around the town of Karatu in Arusha Region.

The Iraqw, also known as the Mbulu or in Kiswahili as Wambulu, are one of Tanzania's larger ethnic groups with a population of around 465,000.

The Isanzu live in Iramba District in Singida Region in central Tanzania. They are one of the smallest groups in the country with a population of about 35,000.

They have had significant influence on the Hadzapi in terms of customs and provision of goods to their neighbours who are hunter-gatherers, unlike the Isanzu who are farmers.

The Jiji, also known as Wajiji, live in Ujiji in Kigoma Region in western Tanzania.

They are a very small group with only about 15,000 and are closely related to the Waha, also known as the Ha, and are even considered to be an integral part of this larger ethnic group. And they speak the Ha language, known as Kiha in Kiswahili.

There's no Jiji language, giving credibility to the argument that they are really part of the Ha ethnic group, even though they are considered to be a distinct group and are indeed identified as a separate ethnic entity may be for historical and cultural reasons.

The Jita live in Mara Region in northern Tanzania on the southern shore of Lake Victoria. They are a fairly large group with a population of about 220,000.

The Kabwa is another ethnic and linguistic group in Mara Region and one of the smallest in the country.

The Kaguru, also known as Kagulu – and as Wakaguru or Wakagulu in Kiswahili – live in central Tanzania. Their population was around 220,000 in 1987 and is probably higher than that today, 20 years later.

The Kahe may be an endangered tribe. There are only

about 3,000 of them and they live southeast of Moshi in northeastern Tanzania.

The Kami live near the city of Morogoro in Morogoro Region in eastern Tanzania. The Kami population is estimated to be around 17,000.

Their language, known as Kikami in Kiswahili, shares many similarities with the Kutu, Kwere, Zaramo, Doe, and Luguru languages spoken by neighbouring tribes in eastern Tanzania.

The Kara are a tribe on Ukerewe Island in Lake Victoria. There are about 90,000 of them. They share the island with the Kerewe.

The Kerewe are one of Tanzania's larger ethnic and linguistic groups with a population of more than 100,000. They live on Ukerewe Island.

The Kimbu live in Chunya District which is in the northern part of Mbeya Region.

Although Mbeya Region is in the southwestern part of the country in the Southern Highlands, Chunya District is close to west-central Tanzania.

There are about 80,000 Kimbus, mostly in Chunya, but some live in different parts of Mbeya Region as well. Another tribe in Chunya District is the Bungu.

Other tribes in Mbeya Region include the Safwa and Malila in Mbeya District, the Nyakyusa in Kyela and Rungwe districts; the Ndali in Ileje District which is their ethnic stronghold just as Rungwe is for the Nyakyusa; the Nyika and the Nyamwanga in Mbozi District; and the Sangu in Mbarali District.

The Kinga live in Njombe District in the Livingstone Mountains northeast of Lake Nyasa.

There are about 150,000 of them and are related to the Nyakyusa just as the Ndali are. I should know – I am a Nyakyusa myself and I know of no evidence which refutes that.

The Kinga also played a major role in the war between the Ngoni and the Nyakyusa.

The Ngoni originally came from Natal Province, South Africa, in the 1830s and settled in Sumbawanga in southwestern Tanzania and in Songea in southeastern Tanzania.

The Ngoni from Songea tried to conquer the Nyakyusa and, to get to Nyakyusaland, they had to cross the Livingstone Mountains where the Kinga lived and where they still live today.

The Kinga were able to warn the Nyakyusa in advance, of the impending invasion by the Ngoni. They also taught the Nyakyusa how to make iron-tipped spears. Before then, Nyakyusa spears were wooden-tipped and were useless against the hard shields used by the Ngoni.

The Nyakyusa did not have any iron-smelting skills until they learnt those skills from their neighbours, the Kinga, with whom they also traded, thus enabling them to make better spears.

But is spite of all those ties, the Nyakyusa had a low opinion of the Kinga. But they once teamed up in a war against the Germans which they lost.

The Ngoni had a reputation as fierce fighters. But they never conquered the Nyakyusa who also had the same reputation as fighters.

From the south we head north where members of one of the smallest ethnic groups in Tanzania live. They are the Kisankasa.

The Kisankasa are of Cushitic origin. And they speak a Cushitic language.

They live in Arusha Region in the northern part of the country. There are about 5,000 of them. That's a very small population.

It may be an endangered tribe like several others in Tanzania because of their very small numbers.

The Kisi are another very small ethnic and linguistic group in Tanzania. There about 20,000 of them.

More than half of them speak the Kisi language, called Kikisi in Kiswahili, and the rest speak Kinyakyusa or

Nyakyusa.

They live on the northeastern shore of Lake Nyasa in Kyela District – which once was part of Rungwe District – and may be related to the Nyakyusa, although their different physical features suggest otherwise.

They began using the Nyakyusa language in the early 1900s and have found it necessary to use it since then because they are far outnumbered by the Nyakyusa in the district.

The men are excellent fishermen.

The Kisi are also known for their pottery. The women are excellent makers of earthenware pots – clay pots – which are used for cooking and storing water.

Kisi men carry the pots as well as fish far inland among the Nyakyusa in Kyela and Rungwe districts – and even far beyond – to sell or exchange them for the goods they need.

The Kisi are also excellent in using canoes to transport people on Lake Nyasa.

Malawians call it Lake Malawi but in Tanzania we call it Lake Nyasa, its original name.

The dispute over the lake – which Malawi claims as its own – has not been settled and remains dormant in a spirit of cooperation and good neighbourliness between the two countries, especially since the end of Dr. Hastings Kamuzu Banda's presidency.

He ruled Malawi with an iron fist and was hostile towards Tanzania. He also claimed huge chunks of Tanzanian territory including the entire region of Mbeya, making things worse.

In the northwestern part of Mbeya Region is Rukwa Region where members of one of Tanzania's relatively small tribes live.

They are members of the Konongo tribe, with a total population of around 52,000. They live in Mpanda District, one of the four districts of Rukwa Region.

Coincidentally, Mbeya and Rukwa are two of the

nation's Big Four regions, so-called because of the large amount of food and other commodities they produce.

Another ethnic and linguistic group is the Kuria. It's one of the larger tribes in Tanzania.

Altogether, there are about 350,000 members of the Kuria tribe in Kenya and Tanzania. The majority of them, about 220,000, live in Tanzania

They straddle the Kenya-Tanzania border and live in Tarime and Serengeti districts in Mara Region in northern Tanzania. In Kenya, they live in Nyanza Province which is in the southwestern part of that country.

The Kuria of Tanzania are both farmers and herders, like their kith-and-kin in Kenya, although they are more pastoralist than their brethren across the border who lean more towards agriculture.

In Tanzania, the Kuria who live in Serengeti District are almost entirely pastoralist.

And the Kuria in both countries are divided into sub-tribes or clans.

The Kutu are an ethnic and linguistic group in Morogoro Region in eastern Tanzania. Their population is about 50,000 and they are one of the few groups that are matrilineal. Most tribes in Tanzania, and elsewhere in Africa, are patrilineal.

The fate of the Kw'adza is one of the tragic stories in Tanzania. They had been an endangered tribe for a long time until they became "extinct."

It was reported in 1999 that their language had become extinct, suggesting that the people themselves had also become extinct.

There are probably some who are still around although there's no credible evidence showing that they still identify themselves as Kw'adza.

Their home was Mbulu District in central Tanzania where the Iraqw, also known as the Mbulu, live. They were distinct from the Iraqw but were related to them.

Their Kw'adza language was in the Afro-Asiatic family

and it was reported that the last speaker of this language died sometime between 1976 and 1999.

The Kwavi are another very small tribe in Tanzania with a very small population. It was reported back in 1957 that there were about 7,378 of them during that time.

They are semi-pastoral and are related to the Maasai who are also pastoralist. They speak the Kwavi language, or Kikwavi as it's known in Kiswahili, and live in Arusha Region in northern Tanzania.

But there's some controversy over their identity. One researcher denies their existence, while another one says the people who are called Ilparakuyo or Baraguyu are Kwavi, implying the terms are synonymous.

The Kwavi are also known as Kwafi and are, in fact, also called Baraguyu.

The Kwaya are yet another very small ethnic and linguistic group in Tanzania. In fact, they're one of the smallest.

They live in Mara Region which borders Kenya and will probably become extinct soon. It was reported in 1987 that there only about 102 of them.

The Kwere are another group that is matrilineal. It's also known as Ngwele.

They live in Bagamoyo District in the coastal region (Pwani) and their population is estimated to be about 100,000. And their primary language is Ngwele.

Bagamoyo also is the home district of Tanzanian President Jakaya Mrisho Kikwete. He's the fourth president and a member of the Kwere tribe.

The Kwifa also known as Kwiva is another very small tribe in Tanzania.

The Lambya is an ethnic and linguistic group in Mbeya Region in southwestern Tanzania. They are also known as Nkoya and live along the Tanzania-Malawi border. There are about 95,000 of them altogether: about 50,000 in Malawi and 45,000 in Tanzania.

A few of them also live in Zambia, a country which

also shares borders with Tanzania and Malawi.

The Luguru are one of the largest ethnic groups in Tanzania. There are about 700,000 of them and they live in Morogoro Region in eastern Tanzania.

They speak the Luguru language, also known as Kiluguru, and the Uluguru Mountains, some of the most well-known in Tanzania, are named after them. They live around the area of Uluguru Mountains near the city of Morogoro.

They are matrilineal and are also known as Ruguru.

The Luo are one of the largest ethnic groups in East Africa. They live mostly in Kenya but a significant number of them also live in Tanzania; and fewer in Uganda.

In Tanzania, they live mostly in Mara Region and straddle the Tanzania-Uganda border.

Some prominent Tanzanian leaders have been Luo, including Timothy Apiyo who was Principal Secretary – Permanent Secretary – in the president's office when Julius Nyerere was president; and Professor Philemon Sarungi who served as Minister of Defence under President Benjamin Mkapa and President Jakaya Kikwete.

The Maasai are one of the most well-known African ethnic groups in the world. Their population is estimated to be about 900,000. About half of them live in Kenya and the other half in Tanzania.

In Tanzania, they live mostly in the northeastern part of the country especially in Arusha and Manyara regions. They also live in north-central Tanzania and many other parts of the country as cattle herders. Many of them also work in towns as security guards because of their reputation as fighters.

They're uncompromising in their defence of their traditional way of life. They are pastoral and semi-nomadic, although some of them have moved to urban centres. And they are the southernmost Nilotic speakers having originally migrated from Sudan and northwestern

Kenya.

The Machinga live in the coastal region of Lindi in southeastern Tanzania. There are about 40,000 of them.

The Magoma are one of Tanzania's smallest ethnic groups. There are about 10,000 of them and they live in Makete District in Iringa Region in the Southern Highlands.

They are often considered to be a sub-group of the Kinga but there are significant differences between the Magoma and the Kinga the languages, thus giving credibility to the argument that the two are different ethnic groups.

The Makonde are one of the largest ethnic and linguistic groups in East Africa. There are about 1.2 million Makonde living in Tanzania, and about 240,000 in Mozambique.

They live throughout Tanzania and Mozambique and a significant number of them also live in Kenya. But their ethnic stronghold is southern Tanzania and across the border in northern Mozambique.

They successfully fought against intruders – African, Arab and European – and were not subjugated until the 1920s by the colonial rulers.

The Makonde are matrilineal.

The Makua also live in southern Tanzania in Mtwara Region, like the Makonde, and are one of Tanzania's larger ethnic groups. They also live in Mozambique.

In fact, they're the largest ethnic group in northern Mozambique. In Tanzania, they live mostly in Masasi District which, coincidentally, is also the home district of former Tanzanian President Benjamin Mkapa.

More than 800,000 Makua live in Mozambique, and more than 360,000 live in Tanzania.

They speak Kimakua.

The Makwe is another tribe straddling the Tanzanian-Mozambican border. There are about 10,000 of them in Tanzania and 22,000 of them in Mozambique.

111

They live along the coast of the Indian Ocean and are one of the smallest ethnic and linguistic groups in Tanzania. They speak Makwe, also known is Kimakwe in Kiswahili. Their language is also known as Maraba or Kimaraba.

The Malila are a tribe in Mbeya Region in the Southern Highlands in the southwestern part of Tanzania. They live in Mbeya District, together with the Safwa who are also indigenous to the district, and other people such as the Nyakyusa who are relatively new comers.

There are about 65,000 Malila in Mbeya District.

The Mambwe are another ethnic and linguistic group in Tanzania. They live in southwestern Tanzania, in Mbeya Region, and in northern Zambia. They straddle the Tanzanian-Zambian border and there about 65,000 of them in Tanzania.

The majority of them live in Zambia where their population is estimated to be about 265,000. They speak Mambwe, or Kimambwe as their language is known in Kiswahili.

The Manda live along the eastern shore of Lake Nyasa in Ludewa District in Iringa Region. There are about 25,000 of them.

The Nyasa also live in the same area and in Songea District as well as other parts of Ruvuma Region.

The Matengo are one of Tanzania's larger ethnic groups. There are about 150,000 of them and they live in Mbinga District in Ruvuma Region. They speak Matengo or Kimatengo.

The Matumbi live in Lindi Region. Their population is estimated to be about 80,000.

The Maviha live along the border with Mozambique in southern Tanzania. They also live in Mozambique. They speak Maviha, or Kimahiva, as their tribal language. They also speak Makua or Kimakua as a second language especially in Mozambique, in addition to Portuguese, the official language of that country.

In Tanzania, they also speak Kiswahili, the national language.

The Mbugwe live in Babati District in north-central Tanzania in Arusha Region. There are about 25,000 of them.

The Mbunga, or Wambunga in Kiswahili, live in Kilombero District in south-central Tanzania in Morogoro Region. There are about 30,000 of them.

The other tribes in Kilombero District are Wapogoro (or Wapogolo) or Pogoro; Wandamba (Ndamba), and Wabena (Bena) although the ethnic stronghold of the Bena is Njombe District in Iringa Region in the Southern Highlands.

The Mosiro are one of the smallest tribes in Tanzania. They are also known as the Akie. Mosiro is an Akie clan name.

The population of the Akie was 5,280 in 2000 and it's highly unlikely that it has grown much.

Like the other hunter-gatherers in Kenya and Tanzania, they are sometimes called Wandorobo in Kiswahili, or Dorobo in English.

Because of their very small population, their future is uncertain and they could become extinct.

The Mpoto live along the northeastern shore of Lake Nyasa in Mbinga District in Ruvuma Region. There are about 90,000 of them.

The Mwanga live in Mbeya Region in southwestern Tanzania and in northern Zambia. Their total population is about 260,000. About 170,000 of them live in Zambia, and 90,000 in Tanzania.

The Mwera are one of the largest ethnic groups in Tanzania. They live in Masasi District in Mtwara Region in southern Tanzania. Some of them also live in Ruvuma and Lindi regions as well as other parts of Tanzania just as many people of other tribes do..

There are more than 470,000 people who belong to the Mwera ethnic and linguistic group. They speak the Mwera

113

language, or Kimwera as it's known in Kiswahili.

The Ndali live in Ileje District in Mbeya Region in southwestern Tanzania. They live in the mountains along the border with Malawi and there about 155,000 of them in Tanzania and about 70,000 in Malawi.

Their Ndali language, or Kindali, is very close to Kinyakyusa or the Nyakyusa language in terms of vocabulary and other linguistic features. Many words are identical. So are the names of the people.

The Ndali, or Wandali, also live in significant numbers in Rungwe District, the homeland of the Nyakyusa, their neighbours. Kyela Disrict is also another Nyakyusaland.

The Ndamba, or Wandamba, live in Kilombero District in Morogoro Region in the south-central eastern part of Tanzania. There are about 85,000 of them.

Their language is similar to Mbunga and Pogoro also known as Pogolo. They are related to the Mbunga and Pogoro tribes who live in the same district. Most of them are Catholic.

The Ndendeule live in Songea and Tunduru districts in Ruvuma Region.

The other tribes in Songea Districts are the Ngoni, Matengo, Yao and Nyasa.

The population of the Ndendeule is around 100,000. And their language, Kindendeule or Kindendeuli, is closest to Kingindo, or Ngindo, which is spoken by members of the Ngindo tribe although they live far away from the Ndendeule in another region and in another part of Tanzania.

The Ndengereko live in Morogoro Region south of the Zaramo River and north of the Rufiji River. There are about 110,000 of them.

They also live in the eastern parts of Songea District in Ruvuma Region.

The Ndonde, also known as Ndonde Hamba, live in southern Tanzania in Nachingwea District in Lindi Region. There are about 20,000 of them.

The Ngasa is a very small ethnic and linguistic group whose members live on the eastern slopes of Mount Kilimanjaro in northeastern Tanzania.

There are about 4,300 of them, and only 200 to 300 Wangasa speak Kingasa, their native language. The rest speak the languages of the dominant tribes around them, including Chaga and Pare, and Kiswahili, the national language.

The Ngoni or Wangoni are one of the most prominent ethnic groups in Tanzania because of their history and legendary role in the Maji Maji war of resistance against the German colonial rulers.

Their home district, Songea in Ruvuma Region in the south part of the country, was the epicentre of this seismic event which shaped Tanzania's history in many fundamental respects.

They are also one of Tanzania's largest ethnic groups whose members also live in all the countries which border Tanzania in the south. There are Ngoni people in Mozambique, Malawi and Zambia.

And they speak Ngoni, or Kingoni as the language is known in Kiswahili. Their language is related to Zulu and other South African languages because of their origin in Natal Province. In fact, Kingoni is a Zulu dialect.

Some of Tanzania's most prominent leaders have been Ngoni, including the country's first vice president, Rashidi Kawawa, who served under Nyerere for decades since independence. He was born and brought up in Songea, the ethnic stronghold of the Ngoni.

Farther north are one of Tanzania's small ethnic groups, the Ngurimi. There are only about 35,000 of them and they live in Mara Region near the border with Kenya. Their language has a lot of similarities with the languages spoken by their neighbours including Ikoma, Zanaki, Kuria, Ikizu, and Gusii, thus suggesting that these are related tribes.

The Nilamba, who are also called Nyilamba, live in

Shinyanga Region in northern Tanzania. They're one of Tanzania's larger ethnic and linguistic groups with a population of about 450,000.

The Nindi are one of the smallest ethnic groups in Tanzania and could become extinct anytime. There are only about 100 of them.

They live in Songea District in Ruvuma Region close to the border with Mozambique. In fact, the group is virtually unknown outside Songea District, yet maintains a distinct identity.

Unfortunately, prospects are bleak that they'll be around for many years to come because of their extremely small number. They're going to die out as an ethnic entity, and some of them will probably be absorbed by other groups through intermarriage and other ways including assimilation.

The Nyakyusa are one of the largest ethnic and lingustic groups in Tanzania and in East Africa.

There are more than 1 million Nyakyusas and their large population has forced many of them to leave their home district of Rungwe and settle in Mbeya District and other parts of the region and elsewhere in Tanzania because of scarcity of land.

They have also settled in other parts of the country in pursuit of different goals including education and careers as well as other interests.

The Nyakyusa were also among the first people in Tanzania to acquire education provided by the missionaries and the colonial government. And because of their early contacts with the European missionaries, mainly German and British, most of them are also Christians. They're mostly Protestant but there are also some Catholics among them.

Their homeland, Rungwe District, is a fertile area of mountains in the Great Rift Valley in the Southern Highlands. The southern part of Rungwe District, Kyela, was once part of Rungwe District. But it's now a separate district. It'ss also a Nyakyusa homeland.

Kyela District is less fertile than the mountainous Rungwe District but it's known throughout the country for its production of rice; while the mountainous Rungwe District is known for its coffee, tea plantations and abundance of bananas and a variety of other crops.

In fact, Rungwe District is the leading producer of food in Mbeya Region and gets large amounts of rain almost throughout the year. It's one of the wettest areas on the entire continent.

The Nyakyusa have lived in this part of the Great Rift Valley for about 500 years. They migrated to the area from Mahenge in Morogoro Region in the eastern part of Tanzania.

And there are more than 300,000 Nyakyusas living in Malawi where they are called Ngonde or Bangonde.

The Nyakyusa of Kyela District are also called Bangonde by the Nyakyusa who live in Rungwe District, although many of them don't like the name. And they call their brethren in the mountainous Rungwe District, Bamwamba, which in Nyakyusa language means "hill people" or "highlanders", a term many northern Nyakyusas don't like either.

The Nyambo are one of Tanzania larger ethnic and linguistic groups who live in Karagwe District in Kagera Region which borders Uganda in northwestern Tanzania. There are more than 400,000 of them.

The Nyanga are another fairly large ethnic group. But most of their members live n Zambia.

There are about 260,000 of them. About 170,000 of them live in northern Zambia and 90,000 in Mbeya Region in southwestern Tanzania.

The Nyamwezi, the second-largest ethnic group after the Sukuma, live mostly in Tabora Region in western Tanzania.

The name of their ethnic group, "Nyamwezi," is of Swahili origin. It means "people of the moon." "Mwezi" means "moon" in Kiswahili. It also means "month."

Their homeland is called Unyawezi and they speak Kinyamwezi.

There are about 2 million of them and they live in many parts of Tanzania, mostly in the western part, but in other regions as well.

The Nyaturu are another large ethnic and linguistic group in Tanzania. They live in Singida Region in north-central Tanzania. There are about 560,000 of them.

The Nyiha live in Mbozi District in Mbeya Region. Their home district borders Zambia. They straddle the Tanzania-Zambia border and are one of Tanzania's larger ethnic groups.

About 310,000 of them live in Tanzania, and more than 320,000 live across the border in Zambia.

The Nyiramba live in Iramba District in Singida Region. Their native language is Kinyiramba and, like most Tanzanians, they also speak Kiswahili, the national language.

The Nyiramba, or Iramba, are one of Tanzania's smaller ethnic and linguistic groups.

Singida, their home region, was once part of the Central Province during British colonial rule in Tanganyika and in the first years of independence until 1963 when all seven provinces were split up and the new administrative units were renamed regions.

The Pangwa live in Ludewa District in Iringa Region in the Southern Highlands. There are about 100,000 of them and they live mainly in the Livingstone Mountains on the eastern shore of Lake Nyasa.

They speak Pangwa which in Kiswahili is known as Kipangwa. The Pangwa themselves call their language Ikipangwa, the first letter "I" being pronounced as an "E" by native English speakers.

The Pare are one of Tanzania's largest ethnic groups. They live in Pare Mountains in Kilimanjaro Region. They speak Pare, or Kipare, but there are ethno-linguistic differences among them.

The Pare who live in the northern part divide their homeland into two areas based on ethno-linguistic differences. Those in the northern part speak Kigweno. And their area is known as Gweno. And those in the southern part speak Kichasu. And their area is known as Usangi.

The entire homeland of the Pare is also generally known as Vuasu.

Same is also their home district. The name of the district is pronounced as *so-* (as in "south") and *ma-* as in ("mango").

The Pare and their neighbours, the Chaga, look very much alike in terms of physical features, a similarity that suggests they are probably related.

They are also related to the Asu people of Kenya, including the Taveta.

Like most Bantu groups, they are patrilineal.

The Pimbwe live in Rukwa Region in southwestern Tanzania close to lake Tanganyika north of Mbeya Region. They are one of the smallest ethnic and linguistic groups in the country and there about 30,000 of them.

The Pogoro, also known as Pogolo, are one of Tanzania's larger ethnic groups. They live in Kilombero District in Morogoro Region and their population is about 200,000.

The Rangi are one of Tanzania's largest ethnic and linguistic groups. The live in Kondoa-Irangi in Dodoma Region in central Tanzania. There are about 360,000 of them and they speak Kilangi, as they language is called. But it's more commonly known as Kirangi.

There are more than 200,000 members of the Rufiji tribe or ethnic group. They live in Rufiji District in Morogoro Region in south-central eastern Tanzania. Their district is named after the name of their tribe. One of Tanzania's main rivers, Rufiji River, is also named after them.

The Rungi live in Rukwa Region on the southeastern shore of Lake Tanganyika . Their population is estimated to be around 170,000.

The Rungu, also known as Lungu, are one of Tanzania's smallest ethnic groups. They live in Mbeya Region in southwestern Tanzania close to the border with Zambia. They also live in northern Zambia.

There are about 40,000 of them in Tanzania. Their population in Zambia has not been independently estimated may be because of their close ties to their neighbours, the Mambwe.

They are related to the Mambwe, one of the largest ethnic groups in Zambia, whose members also live in significant numbers in Mbeya Region in Tanzania.

Their language, Lungu or Kilungu or Chilungu, is almost identical to Kimambwe or Chimambwe, the language spoken by the Mambwe with only minor dialectical differences, suggesting they are basically the same people.

Altogether, the Lungu and the Mambwe constitute a significant population of about 270,000 in Zambia, with the majority of them being Mambwe. This figure suggests that there are probably more Lungu people who live in Tanzania than those who do in Zambia.

The Rungwa are one of the smallest tribes in Tanzania. There are about 20,000 of them and they live in Mpanda District in Rukwa Region in western Tanzania.

The Rwa, or Warwa, live around Mount Meru in Arusha Region. There are about 100,000 of them.

The Safwa are indigenous to Mbeya District in Mbeya Region in the Southern Highlands.

They are one of Tanzania's largest ethnic and linguistic groups with a population of more than 300,000, mostly in Mbeya District. They speak Kisafwa which has a number of dialects including Mbwila, Songwe, Guruka, and Poroto.

And the mountains around the city of Mbeya are

known as Poroto Mountains.

The Safwa are related to the Nyika and the Wanda. Their powerful neighbours, the Sangu also known as Wasangu, conquered them but they were not easy to control.

The Sagala, also known as Sagara, live in central Tanzania. Their population is estimated to be around 85,000.

The Sandawi live in Kondoa District in Dodoma Region in central Tanzania. There are about 40,000 of them.

The Khoi of southern Africa probably migrated from the area of what is Sandawi and Hadzapi territory today in central Tanzania.

There are also a lot of similarities between these ethnic groups in terms of physical features. And the languages of the Sandawi and the Khoi use click sounds. In fact, some research shows that the Khoi migrated from what is Tanzania today.

The Sangu live in Mbeya Region and are one of Tanzania's ethnic groups with a reputation as fierce fighters. There are about 80,000 of them.

They are related to the Nguni of southern Africa.

The Sambaa are one of Tanzania's largest ethnic and linguistic groups. They call themselves Shambaa. They are also known as Sambara or Sambala, and their population is estimated to be around 670,000.

They speak Kishambaa, as the Shambaa or Sambaa call their language, and they live in Usambara Mountains, some of the most fertile parts in Tanzania.

They call their lands Shambalai, a term similar to the Swahili word *shamba* which means "farm." And they are related to the Bondei and the Zigua with whom they have intermarried for a long time.

All these groups are indigenous to Tanga Region in northeastern Tanzania, and their tribal homelands overlap, enabling the people to interact even more.

121

The Usambara Mountains were a favourite area for German settlers who used it for a retreat during the hot season.

And the name Tanganyika, which was the name of the country before it united with Zanzibar to form Tanzania in 1964, may have come from the Sambaa language, or Kisambaa.

It's said that in Kisambaa or Kishambaa, "Tanga" means "farmed land," and "nyika" means "brushy land."Hence Tanga-nyika or Tangayika, the former name of what is now Tanzania mainland.

The Shubi live in Kagera Region in northwestern Tanzania. There are about 160,000 of them.

The Sizaki live near Lake Victoria also in Kagera Region. Their population was estimated to be around 90,000 in 2008.

The Sonjo live in northern Tanzania between 30 and 40 miles west of Lake Natron. They are believed to have lived there for centuries, surrounded by the Maasai who migrated to the region from Kenya and from even farther north in Sudan before they moved into Kenya.

The Sonjo are also known as the Temi. And they call themselves Batemi. In Kiswahili, they are called Watemi. And they call their language Ketemi or Gitemi.

The name Sonjo, or Wasonjo in Kiswahili, was given to them by their powerful neighbours, the Maasai.

They are one of Tanzania's smallest ethnic and linguistic groups with a population of only about 35,000 today.

They are also known for their highly developed traditional irrigation system, an innovation which has led some historians to speculate that the settlement at Engartuka, which had a very developed irrigation system a long time ago and which is one of the nation's most important historical sites, may have a direct connection to these people.

Engartuka is located about 60 miles southeast of Sonjo

country or Batemiland.

The abandoned ruins at Engartuka famous for their ingenious and highly developed cultivation system were once a settlement established by a Bantu group during the Iron Age in the 15th century.

It had a population of several thousand people who developed an intricate irrigation and cultivation system, involving a stone-block canal channelling water from the "Crater Highlands" rift escarpment to stonelined cultivation terraces.

The settlement was abandoned in the mid-1800s. And it's one of the most important archaeological sites on the entire continent.

Another ethnic and linguistic group in Tanzania is the Suba.

The Suba live in Tarime District in Mara Region. There are about 80,000 of them and they speak a number of Suba dialects which are mutually intelligible.

And one of the Suba sub-groups, the Rieri, also speak Luo and may be in the process of adopting it as their primary language.

There are other Suba people who also speak Luo which is the primary language of the Luo who straddle the Kenya-Tanzania border and who live in Mara Region more than they do anywhere else in Tanzania.

The Sumbwa are one of Tanzania's larger ethnic groups who live in Bukombe District in Shinyanga Region. There are about195,000 of them.

The Tongwe live in Kigoma District in western Tanzania. Their population is aorund 32,000.

The Tumbuka is one of the major ethnic and linguistic groups in east-central Africa.

There is no presence of the Tumbuka in Tanzania as an ethnic entity. But because of their geographical location, and proximity to Tanzania, it has been assumed that they also live in Tanzania as an ethnic group.

There are some who do, but only as individuals and

families just like other people do, and not as a distinct entity.

There are about 1.4 million Tumbukas. They live in northern Malawi and eastern Zambia, a region close to Tanzania, leading to speculation that they live in all three countries as an ethnic and linguistic group.

Most of them, about 1 million, live in Malawi and about 400,000 live in Zambia.

One of Tanzania's smallest ethnic and linguistic group is the Vidunda who live in east-central Tanzania. They are matrilineal, unlike most Bantu groups and there about 35,000 of them.

The Vinza is an smaller ethnic and linguistic group with only about 10,000. They live in western Tanzania. Their home district is Uvinza, and they speak Kivinza.

The Wanda live in southwestern Tanzania. There are about 30,000 of them.

The Wanji live in Kipengere Mountains in Makete District in Iringa Region in the Southern Highlands. Their population is estimated to be around 30,000.

The Ware are believed to be extinct. Their homeland was an island in Tanzanian waters in the eastern part of Lake Victoria and it's not known whether there are still any people who identify themselves as Ware on that island or anywhere else.

The Yao are one of the largest ethnic and linguistic groups in Tanzania. They live mostly in Mtwara Region, and in significant numbers in Ruvuma Region, in southern Tanzania. And they straddle the border between Tanzania and Mozambique. They also live in Malawi.

About half a million of them live in Tanzania; another half a million in Mozambique, and about one million in Malawi – mostly in the southern part of the country.

Their language is Chiyao, as they call it, or Kiyao as it's known in Kiswahili. And their traditional homeland is between Ruvuma River and Lugenda River in northern Mozambique.

They have a strong cultural identity which transcends national boundaries, clearly demonstrated by the cultural unity that exists among them in all the three countries in which they live.

The Zanaki are an ethnic and linguistic group in Mara Region in northern Tanzania. There are about 65,000 of them and they live mostly in Musoma District.

Tanzania's first president, Julius Nyerere, was a Zanaki. He came from Butiama village in Musoma District and was buried in his home village after he died in October 1999.

The Zaramo are one of the largest ethnic and linguistic groups in Tanzania. There are about 660,000 of them and they live mainly in the area between Dar es Salaam and Bagamoyo on the east coast.

The Zigua are another large ethnic group in Tanzania. Their population is estimated to be around 360,000 and they live in a coastal area between Dar es Salaam and Tanga. They are also one of the main ethnic and linguistic groups in Tanga Region.

The Zinza live on the southwestern shore of Lake Victoria and on nearby islands. Their population is estimated to be around 145,000.

The Zyoba, or Joba, live in western Tanzania near Lake Tanganyika and are one of the smallest ethnic and linguistic groups in the country. They also live across the lake in the Democratic Republic of Congo (DRC).

What emerges from this survey of Tanzania's demographic landscape is that most of the tribes or ethnic groups in Tanzania are small with fewer than 100,000 people each. And this demographic composition has played a critical role in the history of the country in terms maintaining peace and stability.

There are no dominant tribes, in terms of population, to exercise a disproportionate influence over the others. And this has been a blessing for Tanzania on a continent wracked by ethnic conflicts through the decades, only in varying degrees.

But the stability of Tanzania as one of the most peaceful countries on the continent and in the entire world is attributable to other factors as well, including national leadership especially under the country's first president, Julius Nyerere, focusing on national unity transcending tribal and regional loyalties.

Also the use of a common language, Kiswahili, which was vigorously promoted across the country to create a sense of national identity, played a major role in uniting Tanzanians of all tribes and races.

No less important were the egalitarian policies and ideals of President Nyerere which emphasised equality across the spectrum.

Without all those factors combined, Tanzania would probably not be what it is today as one of the most stable, most peaceful, and most united countries in the world. And it has enjoyed peace and stability since independence and even before then; a rare achievement on this turbulent continent.

In terms of culture, all the members of Tanzania's black African ethnic groups or tribes, and racial minorities – mostly Asian, especially of Indian and Pakistani origin, Arab, and European, mainly British – have their own distinct cultures handed down through the generations and shaped by different historical experiences.

Yet, there are many things which Tanzanians have in common and which collectively constitute a national culture and even character.

But equally important are the different cultures of different tribes and racial minorities in different parts of the country.

One of the most interesting groups are the Swahili. They are an eclectic blend or mixture of Arabs and an assortment of indigenous black African groups.

There are also elements of other groups, especially Persian, among the Swahili.

126

And they all, through the centuries, have blended and created one of the most dynamic cultures in history. They have also produced a new language which is older than modern English.

They are called Waswahili or Swahili. And they speak a language called Kiswahili or Swahili. And their culture is also Swahili culture.

They live mostly along the coast but, through the years, many of them have also moved into the interior and settled mostly in towns in different parts of the country.

They also transcend national boundaries in terms of identity as a cultural group and are in inextricably linked with the Swahili in Kenya constituting an organic whole virtually indistinguishable from each other.

And they are the focus of an appendix in this book as a group representative of Tanzania in many fundamental respects, including the country's ability to transcend ethnic and tribal divisions and its unique attribute as a nation united by a common African language unlike anywhere else on this fractured continent whose countries are divided along ethno-regional lines with the exception of a few.

Among those very few exceptions is Tanzania, a country which came into being when Tanganyika united with Zanzibar in April 1964.

We look at that union, and the problems it faces among other subjects, in the next chapter.

Chapter Six:

The Union of Tanganyika and Zanzibar

THE Union of Tanganyika and Zanzibar was formed on 26 April 1964 when the two countries united to form one country. It was named the United Republic of Tanzania on 29 October the same year.

Both were independent countries. And both ceased to exist as countries when the union was formed. They surrendered their sovereignties to a higher authority, the state of Tanzania, which was the product of the union.

It was the first union of independent countries ever formed on the African continent. And it's the only union of independent states that exists on the continent today.

It is a peculiar union, unique in its configuration in the entire world.

While both Tanganyika and Zanzibar ceased to exist as

separate nations and as countries, Zanzibar retained its status and continued to exist as a political entity, but not as an independent state. Tanganyika, on the other hand, ceased to exist even as a political entity. There is no Tanganyika today. And there are no Tanganyikans. But there is Zanzibar, and there are Zanzibaris.

This unique arrangement was deliberately crafted to ensure that Zanzibar retained its identity in the larger political entity of the union in order to alleviate fears among Zanzibaris that they had been swallowed up by Tanganyika.

The president of Zanzibar, Abeid Karume, wanted a complete merger. But the president of Tanganyika, Julius Nyerere, refused. He did not think it was a good idea for Zanzibar to lose its identity completely because Tanganyika was much bigger than Zanzibar, in terms of area and population, and felt there was an imperative need to assure Zanzibaris that they had not been submerged in the merger.

But in spite of that guarantee, many Zanzibaris felt back then, and still fee today, that they were not treated fairly when the union was formed. They feel that when their country united with Tanganyika, it became a junior partner in the union.

And there are those who contend that Zanzibar entered the union as an independent state and never lost its status as a sovereign nation. There are also many Zanzibaris who simply don't want to be part of the union. They say it was a mistake from the beginning for the two countries to unite and Zanzibar has not benefited from the merger.

In 2000, Seif Shariff Hamad, the leader of the Civic United Front (CUF) which is Tanzania's largest opposition party, bluntly stated that if his party won the election in Zanzibar, he would lead Zanzibar out of the union. The Civic United Front is strongest in Zanzibar, especially on Pemba Island.

There are also complaints from the mainland. Former

Tanganyikans, now Tanzania mainlanders as opposed to Zanzibar islanders, say the former island nation is overly represented in the union government and other state organs despite its size which is much smaller than that of former Tanganyika.

Also a group of 55 members of parliament from the mainland supported a bill in the 1990s which would have established a separate government for Tanganyika. They wanted Tanzania to have three governments: one for the union, one for Zanzibar, and one for Tanganyika or Tanzania mainland.

The founder of the union, Julius Nyerere although no longer president of Tanzania, was totally against the idea and said restructuring the union on the basis of three governments would destroyed the union.

He still had formidable influence after he stepped down from the presidency and remained the most powerful national leader until his death in October 1999 at the age of 77.

The the fate of the union again became a subject of public debate in June-July 2008 when Tanzania's Prime Minister Mizengo Pinda said in parliament that Zanzibar was not a country and ceased to exist as a sovereign nation when it united with Tanganyika in 1964. He was answering a question by a member of parliament from Zanzibar who wanted to know whether or not Zanzibar was still a country.

His response sparked furious debate in Zanzibar, and even in the Zanzibar legislature, with many Zanzibaris maintaining that Zanzibar was indeed a country and never lost its status as as an independent nation. There were also demonstrations in Zanzibar against what the prime minister said in parliament.

The matter was widely covered by the Tanzanian media. It also got attention from other East African media outlets, especially in Kenya and Uganda whose leaders have discussed with their counterparts in Tanzania the possibility of forming an East African federation under one government. As one of the Tanzanian newspapers, *The Citizen*, Dar es Salaam, stated in its report of 26 July 2008 from Zanzibar entitled "Shamhuna Adamant Over Zanzibar Status":

" The debate about Zanzibar's sovereignty once again emerged in the House of Representatives yesterday with the Isles' government vowing to stick to its earlier stance.

Apparently defying calls to shelve the debate on grounds that the union government was handling the issue, a senior Zanzibar Government official said the debate was far from over.

He suggested that they were determined to defend their view on the political status of the Isles despite the fact that their Constitution and that of the United Republic clearly state that Zanzibar is part of Tanzania.

Speaking in the House yesterday, the Isles' deputy chief minister, Mr Ali Juma Shamhuna, denounced claims that Zanzibar is part of Tanzania.

He was responding to contributions by members of the House of Representatives when discussing the 2008/9 Budget speech for the Ministry of Information, Culture and Sports.

Mr Shamhuna said Zanzibar was a sovereign state and would continue to hold that political status forever.

'The subject of whether or not Zanzibar is a sovereign state has not been exhaustively discussed. And I think we have the right to continue discussing it,' he said.

Recently, the speaker of the House banned the debate saying Prime Minister Mizengo Pinda's office was handling the issue.

The prime minister has ordered the attorney-generals from the Mainland and Zanzibar to find a way of clearing any doubt over the political status.

Mr Pinda said he believed the problem originated from different interpretations of the Constitution. 'It might be better for attorney-generals from both sides to look into it and, if necessary, give proposals on how to solve it,' he said.

But Mr Shamhuna told the (Zanzibar) House that there was no question about the Isles' status.

He said: 'Zanzibar is a sovereign state and it will continue retaining such a status. We should not get tired of defending such a status.'

The chief minister referred to Article 9 of Zanzibar's Constitution arguing that it provided a clear picture of the Isles' status. 'The fact that Zanzibar has its own executive, legislature and judiciary substantiates that it is a state on its own,' he said.

Mr Shamhuna, who is also the Minister for Information, Culture and Sports, said he was surprised by those who issued statements claiming that Zanzibar was not a sovereign state. He added that no one had the authority to stop the people of Zanzibar from fighting for their rights.

'Currently, countries almost all over the world are transforming themselves into more democratic states. In doing so, people in those countries no longer fear anyone when fighting for their rights,' said Mr Shamhuna.

His remarks were a veiled attack on some senior Government officials who had been reportedly trying to convince people not to discuss the subject on grounds that it constituted treason.

He also said he agreed with the statement given earlier by Zanzibar Attorney-General (AG) Iddi Pandu Hassan in which the AG described Mr Pinda's remarks in the (Tanzania) National Assembly recently as 'a slip of the tongue.'

The minister explained that the prime minister's remarks in Dodoma had actually increased the people's desire to discuss the matter.

'We thought the statement made by the Attorney-General on behalf of the Zanzibar Government that refuted the Prime Minister's utterances was clear and that the statement by Mr Pinda was just a slip of the tongue.

'But since the prime minister has stuck to his earlier statement, we are made to believe that this debate is not over,' he said.

Mr Shamhuna said officials who were threatening people over the subject were undemocratic.

Since last month when the controversy surfaced, there had been calls for authorities to settle the matter that threatens the fragile union government.

But his (Prime Minister Pinda's) stance that the Isles is not an independent country outside the union government within which it can only exercise its sovereignty has apparently earned him a lot of criticism from the Zanzibar House of Representatives."

The speaker of the union parliament, Samwel Sitta, also banned the debate on Zanzibar's status in the union. According to a report in another Tanzanian newspaper, *The Guardian*, 25 July 2008, from the nation's capital Dodoma, entitled "Sitta Also Bans Debate on Zanzibar Status":

"National Assembly Speaker Samwel Sitta issued a directive here yesterday effectively barring Members of Parliament from any further discussion on whether Zanzibar is legally a state....

The Speaker explained that the Prime Minister elaborated comprehensively on the issue inside the House last week, including recommending that the Union and Zanzibar attorney generals pursue it jointly to its logical conclusion....

He stood by his ruling amid a wave of questions on what the Union Constitution said about the status of the Isles from the opposition camp, led by Zanzibar legislators Mohamed Habib Mnyaa (Mkanyageni - CUF) and Dr Ali Tarab Ali (Konde - CUF) .

Mnyaa had demanded explanation from the Prime Minister on whether it was the Articles of Union that formed the United Republic of Tanzania or the Union Constitution that reigned supreme.

'I think Hon Mnyaa is not wishing me any good. I didn't want to comment on this issue at length. I have learned from the media that there was a demo planned against me in Zanzibar,' noted Pinda, before responding.

He then said the matter had already been left in the hands of the two attorney generals in the hope that they would make a thorough study of the Constitution and see where there were problems and how best to deal with them.

He added that he believed time had come for the ruling CCM to take up the matter and issue a conclusive statement on it 'after which I think we will be in a position to get a definitive answer.'

'Since the Union belongs to all Tanzanians, the issue is not the responsibility of only the government but of all the people,' argued the legislator, his favourite option being the initiation of a public dialogue 'so that the people can decide.'

It was at that juncture that Speaker Sitta intervened, issuing the 'stop order' just as Zanzibar House of Representatives Speaker Pandu Ameir Kificho did only days ago.

Responding to MPs' questions in the National Assembly last week, the Prime Minister was emphatic that there was no way Zanzibar could become a sovereign state within another sovereign state (the United Republic of Tanzania) because doing that would automatically break the April 26, 1964 Union between Tanganyika and Zanzibar.

Pinda, a lawyer, explained that Zanzibar was not a sovereign state because it lost the status when it became part of a new sovereign state known as the United Republic of Tanzania.

He said he saw no way during his prime ministerial tenure in which he would be a party to a political experience or process that would lead to the collapse of 'the precious and exemplary Union between Tanganyika and Zanzibar.'"

There are leaders on both sides who want to preserve the union. But no-one knows if the union would survive if the people were asked to decide in a referendum on Africa's only union of independent states – whether or not it should continue to exist.

In spite of the problems the union faces, there's no question that it has survived, and even thrived, for more than 40 years since its consummation in 1964. And Tanzania has, throughout its history, been one of the most stable and most peaceful countries on the continent and in the entire world.

So, if the merger were a threat to national stability and security, its existence for more than four decades as a stable entity provides incontrovertible evidence showing that is not the case.

Also the majority of Tanzanians, on the mainland and in the isles, were born after the union was formed. Tanzania is the only country they know. And it's highly unlikely that the majority of them would want it to break up.

They know nothing from personal experience, like their parents do, about the existence of Tanganyika and Zanzibar as separate nations. And it is Tanzanians of this generation in whose hands lies the future of the union.

Should their parents succeed in breaking up the union, although this is only a remote possibility, they would have betrayed their own children whose destiny is inextricably linked with the continued existence of Tanzania as a single political entity under one government of this United Republic.

However, it must also be emphasised that there are

many people of the younger generation on both sides of the union – in Zanzibar and on the mainland – who want the union dissolved. Many people on the mainland, younger and older ones, feel that Zanzibar is burden on them. The former island nation does not have a lot of resources and is dependent on the mainland for economic survival.

Many Zanzibaris, of all generations, contend otherwise. They say they are exploited by the mainland.

The debate on the status of Zanzibar in the union escalated in August 2008 when legislators from Zanzibar and from the mainland had a heated exchange in the national parliament, with some of the MPs (members of parliament) calling for the restructuring of the union on the basis of three governments, including one for the mainland.

Currently, Tanzania mainland does not have a separate government. There are only two governments: one for Zanzibar and one for the union which also serves the mainland.

Others wanted to have only one government for the whole country: none for Zanzibar and none for the mainland.

And there were some MPs from Zanzibar who bluntly stated that the union should be dissolved and the former island nation should reclaim its former status it once enjoyed as a full sovereign entity.

According to a report on the parliamentary proceedings in Dodoma published in *The Citizen*, Dar es Salaam, 21 August 2008, entitled "Mainland, Z'bar Mps Disagree":

"The debate over Zanzibar's status raged in Parliament yesterday with legislators from the Mainland calling for the formation of a single government as the permanent solution to conflicts arising from the current union structure.

While Zanzibar MPs continued to pour scorn on the

structure of the Union and pressed for a review of the constitution, Mainland MPs took the view that the formation of one government was the answer to the growing crisis over the status of Zanzibar in the union government.

The House was debating the budget estimates tabled by the Minister of State in Vice President's Office responsible for Union Affairs, Mr Muhammad Seif Khatib, who was seeking the approval of Sh2.3 billion for the ministry.

Unlike the division that emerged in the House when debating the proposal to set up Kadhi courts in which MPs were divided along religious lines, this time CCM and CUF MPs from the Isles buried their differences. They expressed dissatisfaction with the union structure while MPs from the Mainland called for a single government.

Before the debate, opposition spokesperson for Union issues, Riziki Juma, said the structure of the union was the first issue to be dealt with if union differences are to be resolved.

She said the Union constitution does not reflect the original Articles of Union as key items had been left out, or were in the constitution but in practice this isn't the case.

The first MP to propose a one-government structure was Mr Lucas Selelii (Nzega-CCM) who told the House that forming one union government was the best answer in solving the growing crisis over the state of the union and the status of Zanzibar.

'I caution that our fellow MPs must know that the union comprises two parts. All of us have a profound interest in it, but I'm surprised by our colleagues' claim that they are sidelined,' he said, underlining that self-sacrifice was paramount for the union to last.

He said differences in the union could be sorted out through existing mechanisms without having to question the union. But Zanzibar MPs continued to pile on accusations that the union favoured Mainlanders.

138

Mr Ali Said Salim (CUF) sought an explanation on the issue of Zanzibar's shares in the Bank of Tanzania, saying Zanzibar has been contributing to the BoT as part of Tanzania but the contribution ended in benefiting only the Mainland.

He said since the union was formed, it was automatic that the sovereignty of the two countries died after the union but the current structure of the union operates as if Zanzibar never existed.

He said that under the original agreement of the union and by the constitution, the Zanzibar President would remain the vice-president but the provision has been flawed and the president is no longer the VP.

He hit back at Kyela MP Harrison Mwakyembe who last week accused Zanzibar ministers of being disrespectful by criticizing Prime Minister Mizengo Pinda for saying Zanzibar was not a state.

The MP said Dr Mwakyembe should apologise to all Zanzibaris, citing Article 103 (3) of the constitution, where Zanzibar ministers are only responsible to the Zanzibar President and that they had the right to express their feelings.

But Mr Selelii quoted article 1 of the Union constitution, its territory and its people, which stipulates that Tanzania is one state and is a sovereign united republic.

Article 2 (1) states that the territory of the United Republic consists of the whole of Mainland Tanzania and the whole area of Tanzania Zanzibar including the territorial waters.

He then quoted article 52 (2) on the powers of the Prime Minister, which notes that the PM shall have authority over the control, supervision and execution of the day to-day function and affairs of government of the United Republic.

'This is enough to prove that the PM has authority on the two sides of the union and that Dr Mwakyembe was right and it is they who are supposed to apologise,' the MP insisted.

Mr Job Ndugai (Kongwa-CCM) said Tanzanians are becoming tired of hearing endless complaints from Zanzibar MP.

He said the Kongwa constituency he represents has 300,000 inhabitants but only one MP while Pemba Island, which has the same number of people, is represented in Parliament by nearly 30 MPs. He said despite such hiccups no MP from the Mainland had ever complained.

He said it was unfair for a minister from the Revolutionary Government of Zanzibar to openly scoff at the PM and blowing minor contentious issues on the Union out of proportion.

To end the emerging problems about the union, having one union government was the only remaining option, he further declared.

Mr Mohamed Amour Chombo (Magomeni-CCM) insisted that the current structure of the union was not beneficial to Zanzibaris and they are the ones who carry the burden caused by existing discrepancies in the union.

He said the best way to help Zanzibar get out of the problem and find ways of boosting its economy was allowing it to join the Organization of Islamic Conference (OIC).

Mr Ponsiano Nyami (Nkasi-CCM) called MPs who stood against the union 'agitators' and that they were not supposed to be in the House. 'The worst thing about this is that it is the MPs who under article 65 of the constitution swore to protect the constitution are the ones abusing it,' he said.

'If you fail to defend the constitution you are no longer eligible to be a member of this House. Go and talk of your anti-union sentiments outside the chamber,' the MP intoned.

He said Zanzibar which has less than one million people has over 50 MPs and five members of the House of

Representative have seats in Parliament. Mainland Tanzania with over 40 million people are represented by just 250 MPs and none of their MPs enters the House of Representatives."

And according to a report in the government-owned newspaper, the *Daily News*, also from the nation's capital Dodoma – seat of the national parliament – published on 21 August 2008 and entitled "MPs Divided Over Union Setup":

"Members of Parliament were yesterday divided on whether the state of the Union should maintain the current two-tier but single Union government or adopt thorny proposals for a three-tier federal system of administration.

The opposition criticized the present two-tier structure of the Union in favour of a federal system with three governments.

Contributing to the budget proposals of the Vice-President's Office (Union Matters), most MPs opposed the proposals for a federal administration and called for a single government instead, arguing it was the ultimate stage of the 44-year-old political marriage between the then Tanganyika and Zanzibar.

But when winding up, the Minister of State in the Vice-President's Office (Union Matters), Mr Muhammed Seif Khatib, said any changes of the Union should come from 'wananchi' themselves, not just Parliament. He said that the Union would be changed to accommodate prevailing changes and to address some challenges when necessary, admitting that the Union was man-made therefore it had some shortcomings.

'There's no need to keep on complaining ... let's come up with strong arguments to make the necessary changes because the Union is dynamic ... A better way of respecting the Union's founders is to consolidate the Union instead of merely showering praises on them,' he noted.

Mr Khatib pointed out to what he described as 'hypocrisy and insufficient knowledge and information' on the Union that had led some leaders to exaggerate all issues touching on the Union.

Earlier on, Mr Lucas Selelii (Nzega – CCM) proposed for a single government, but appealed for tolerance and constructive dialogue to maintain the 44-year-old Union. The legislator expressed deep concern over recent exchanges of heated swipes between politicians, including those traded between ministers from the two sides of the Union.

He said the political marriage between the then Tanganyika and Zanzibar was not ordained by divine law, saying it was the product of human beings with inherent shortcomings that could be amicably resolved through dialogue and consensus.

Mr Mudhihir Mudhihir (Mkinga – CCM) and Mr Ponsian Nyami also called for a single government structure, but warned that there were people who were distorting facts on the Union leading to confusion.

'With one government in place, there will be no complaints,' Mr Nyami told the House.

Mr Mudhihir noted that process to form one government should be a gradual, peaceful, cohesive ... not forceful one.

'Any effective medicine is bitter ... it is not easy to go away with Zanzibar government due to the traditions...one government is the only solution,' he said.

Mr Mudhihir said there were claims that there was no revolution in Zanzibar on January 12, 1964, but that people from the then Tanganyika invaded the Isles and toppled the government in power.

'This is not true at all,' the MP said, referring to a book by an author called Feruz. The legislator described the book as 'a collection of lies' and charged that the author was among people who had attempted to distort the history of the Union.

The MP said the author listed the alleged invaders from Tanganyika as Mr Hassan Nassor Moyo, Mr Abdallah Natepe, Mr Said Mfaranyaki and one Mr Darwesh.

Ms Riziki Omar Juma (Special Seats – CUF) told the House late Tuesday that the current structure was among the causes of discontentment in the country.

Ms Juma, who is the opposition spokesperson on Union Affairs, also charged that some of the changes in the Constitution of the United Republic of Tanzania of 1977, were against the letter and spirit of the original 1964 Articles of Union.

The opposition contended that the Articles of the Union provided that the Chairman of the Zanzibar Revolutionary Council and Isles President was then designated the Union Vice-President.

She said that under the present arrangement, the president of Zanzibar was a mere member of the Union cabinet, with insignificant authority over affairs on the United Republic.

The MP also challenged continued extension of the Union matters in the first schedule of the Constitution from the original 11 items to 22 at present.

She said many of the additional items were not in favour of the Isles – citing the position of the Attorney General of the United Republic as 'unconstitutional' since the administration of justice was not a union matter.

During debate on the 2008/09 budget proposals for the Vice-President's Office, the Minister of State in the Prime Minister's Office (Parliamentary Affairs), Mr Philip Marmo, said all constitutional changes were supported by legislators from Zanzibar.

'It is unfair to blame legislators from the Mainland on the changes because the Zanzibar House of Representatives and the Union Parliament unanimously endorsed them,' he said when he rose on the point of information."

143

Tanzania's President Jakaya Kikwete bluntly stated that both Tanganyika and Zanzibar surrendered their sovereignties when they united in 1964 to form one country known as Tanzania.

By saying so, he threw his weight behind Prime Minister Mizengo Pinda who had been had been harshly criticised by many Zainzibaris for saying that Zanzibar no longer exists as a sovereign state but is an integral of the United Repubic of Tanzania. According to a report in one of Tanzania's leading newspapers, *The Guardian*, from the nation's capital Dodoma, 22 August 2008, entitled "JK Irked by Union Debate":

"Debate on whether Zanzibar is a state or not is unfortunate because it is propagated by the same people charged with the responsibility of advising the government, President Jakaya Kikwete said yesterday.

Addressing Parliament, Kikwete hit out at public leaders who he said confused the wananchi deliberately on the issue of the structure of the union between Tanganyika and Zanzibar.

In his three-hour speech, President Kikwete said he did not believe that after 44 years of the Union, there were public leaders who did not know the essence and history of the Union.

'We are confusing and dividing our people for nothing. There is no need to show our differences on this issue in public. It is unfortunate that some of the people behind this issue are members of the committees formed to work on the problems of the union, he said.

The President said both Tanganyika and Zanzibar surrendered their sovereignty in 1964 to give way to a new sovereign state, which is Tanzania.

'Tanzania is the new sovereign state which identifies the people of Tanganyika and Zanzibar,' he said, adding, maybe the people behind this issue have their own agenda.

Otherwise I see nothing which the people do not understand.'

The President said Tanzania was still one country and the Union was still strong.

'There have been some challenges, but every time they arise, we have been working on them using the system we have put in place to solve our problems,' he said.

Kikwete said even the wave of arguing whether Zanzibar was a country or not would pass. He called on public leaders to avoid using languages that might divide the people.

He said the teams formed to work on the problems of the Union were going on well, adding that he was optimistic that the solution would be found.

There has of late been a debate on the status of Zanzibar in the Union government, following Prime Minister Mizengo Pinda's statement in Parliament last month that Zanzibar is not a state.

Pinda's statement sparked debate in the House of Representatives with some Zanzibar government ministers saying the PM was wrong.

On Wednesday, the House was divided on the issue of the structure of the Union, with legislators from Zanzibar demanding a new set up that would benefit both sides."

An editorial in the same newspaper captured the essence of the controversy and expounded on some of the themes which have been the subject of debate between Tanzanians who support the union and those who are opposed to the merger. Published in *The Guardian*, 23 August 2008, the editorial was headlined, "What's Behind Zanzibar Debate?":

"For quite some time, the issue of sovereignty of Zanzibar has dominated print and electronic media highlights. The whole controversy surfaced from nowhere other than inside the Union legislature itself.

145

It all began during a question and answer session, when the Prime Minister, in an answer to a question as to whether Zanzibar was a country or not, said that the country's sovereignty, including that of Zanzibar, rested in the United Republic of Tanzania.

This statement was sufficient to provoke a furore that culminated in President Jakaya Kikwete's speech in Dodoma on Thursday, who said that he did not believe that after 44 years of the Union, there were political leaders who did not know the essence and history of the Union.

The President said that both Tanganyika and Zanzibar surrendered their sovereignty in 1964 to give way to a new state, which is Tanzania. He added that Tanzania was the new state which identified the people of Tanganyika and Zanzibar.

Much as we agree that the concept of sovereignty is a playfield of political scientists, it basically revolves around the fact that there must be a supreme power existing in a state, and in this case, the United Republic of Tanzania, although Zanzibar has retained a significant degree of autonomy.

At the centre of the whole debate is the validity of the word 'country,' as could be applied to Zanzibar in its current constitutional status.

Currently, Zanzibar has its own anthem, legislature and autonomous government, which runs several ministries apart from those which fall under the auspices of the Union government, which also comprises cabinet ministers from Zanzibar.

This is more or less similar with the United Kingdom of Great Britain and Northern Ireland, commonly called Great Britain or Britain.

According to a dictionary definition, Britain is described as 'a country of Western Europe comprising England, Scotland, Wales and Northern Ireland.'

Likewise, Tanzania, a unitary state, is a country in

Eastern Africa, comprising Tanganyika and Zanzibar, so the supreme power of this country lies neither in Tanganyika nor Zanzibar but in the government of the United Republic of Tanzania.

Granted that Zanzibar has got a government, House of Representatives and its own anthem and constitution, so have the constituent states and provinces in the federal systems of Australia, Canada and the United States and Union of South Africa.

As in any state merger, the United Republic of Tanzania is not a Union without problems.

Such problems can relate to the devolution of powers and challenges of upholding not only the letter, but also the spirit of the Articles of the Union.

Other challenges of the Union include primordial tendencies, which could also be at the heart of the on-going controversy.

For that reason, it is better for holders of such views to come out in the open and profess their true intentions so that the whole issue can be debated and acted upon not only in a transparent manner, but also in line with the country's Constitution."

The debate over the status of Zanzibar underscores one fundamental fact: There are a number of issues which have not been resolved or clarified since the union was formed in 1964.

And one of the ways to address those issues is by encouraging public discussion on the nature of the union and its shortcomings, not just its advantages.

So far, the discussion has focused on the advantages of the union. To make it stronger and durable, its weaknesses must be exposed and corrected.

One of those issues is the number of governments the union should have.

Should it have just one government? Or should it have two – one for Zanzibar and one for the union which also

147

functions as the government for Tanzania mainland? Or should it have three governments – one for the union, one for Zanzibar, and one for Tanganyika as some members of parliament from the mainland and former First Vice President of the United Republic, Aboud Jumbe, a Zanzibari, as well as others from both the mainland and the isles suggested?

When the union was formed, it was formed by two governments – the government of Tanganyika and the government of Zanzibar – representing two independent states.

And the union still has two governments today, although Tanganyika does not have one since it does not exist as a political entity. But there are two political entities, the United Republic and Zanzibar, and each has its own government although the union government has jurisdiction over Zanzibar on union matters.

The union government also functions as the government for Tanzania mainland, what was once known as Tanganyika.

If the union had three governments – one for the United Republic, one for Zanzibar, and one for Tanganyika – then the country would have three political entities, not two which originally formed the union.

It would be a union of three political entities, a union which was originally formed by only two, Tanganyika and Zanzibar; the third political entity – the United Republic – being a product f the original two.

Was the purpose of the union to create three political entities or one?

The two which exist today, the United Republic and Zanzibar, are intended to maintain the union, and not to legitimise the existence of two separate countries – the United Republic and Zanzibar.

That is because there is only one country in the union. And that is Tanzania.

But those are some of the issues we Tanzanians have

148

not discussed thoroughly through the years since the union was formed about 45 years ago.

Although the union has survived for almost 50 years – close to half a century ! - thus attesting to its strength in spite of the rocky relationship between Zanzibar and the mainland in a number of areas through the years, there are those who contend that it's in danger of collapsing and could collapse anytime because of its inherent weaknesses. Some of those weaknesses are attributed to its structural flaws.

But they can be corrected if the union is restructured to accommodate conflicting interests on an equitable basis far more than it does now.

The restructuring of the union may include extensive devolution of power to the regions, especially the regions in the former island nation of Zanzibar, or a centralised state – as it exists now – which allows a lot more freedom to Zanzibaris to manage their own affairs with very little involvement of the union government.

Some people, especially Zanzibaris, say the union could collapse because the former island nation hardly gets any benefits from the merger.

They also contend that Zanzibar is deliberately ignored by the central government in the allocation of funds and other resources, an injustice they say justifies secession and dissolution of the union.

And there are those who simply don't want the union. They come from both sides – Zanzibar and the mainland – although sentiments for ending the union are much stronger among Zanzibaris than they are among Tanzania mainlanders.

But whatever strengths the union has which justify its continued existence, and whatever weaknesses it has which may justify its dissolution or secession of Zanzibar, the question that continues to haunt the nation is whether or not the merger is really getting weaker and weaker or getting stronger. As Professor Haroub Othman, a

Zanzibari, teaching at the University of Dar es Salaam on the mainland, stated in a series of articles in one of Tanzania's newspapers, *The Guardian*, Dar es Salaam, on the 40th anniversary of the union, entitled, "Tanzania: Forty Years of the Union: Is it Withering Away?":

"In the last forty years, Tanzanians have prided themselves in having the only union of independent states in Africa; and even though no other states have followed their example, they have not been discouraged by this lack of interest in forging larger units in Africa; nor do they think there were any lessons to be drawn form the failures of such attempts elsewhere.

But now cracks are appearing, without any obvious prodding form outside....

The Union is a fact. Despite a lot of problems, it has brought stability and peace in the region.

It is difficult to speculate what would have happened to the Zanzibar Revolution without the Union: whether Zanzibar would have advanced faster or whether a counter-revolutionary force would have taken over and embellished a dictatorship worse than anything the islands have actually experienced especially during the first phase government.

It is difficult to speculate what would have happened to the Zanzibar Revolution without the Union: whether Zanzibar would have advanced faster or whether a counter-revolutionary force would have taken over and embellished a dictatorship worse than anything the islands have actually experienced especially during the first phase government.

What is clear though is that the Union has brought the two peoples much closer together.

I do not believe that the unity of the two peoples can be strengthened by restructuring the present set-up into a federation.

150

I see movement from the present set-up to a federation as a step towards the dismemberment of the Union; and I do not think that that is to the short- or long-term benefit of the people of Tanzania.

The present problems can be resolved if there is a strong political will on the part of our political class and if the people are told the truth about those problems.

Only when corrective measures are taken, would it be possible to sustain and strengthen the Union. Otherwise if the difficulties inherent in the 'Articles of Union' and the problems arising from implementation are only emphasized and not resolved, the tendency would be towards the withering away of the Union.

In this era of multipartism and openness, it is even more important that matters are discussed and solutions founded on popular will.

Of all the political parties that have been established since the abolition of the one-party system, only one, the Democratic Party led by Reverend Christopher Mtikila, has come out strongly against the Union and called for its dissolution.

Others are prevaricating between 'referendum', 'federation' and modifications within the present set-up. The CCM and its governments...now seems to be torn apart, with a strong group calling for a federal set-up.

The national language, the ethics of equality and human dignity, and the Union of Tanganyika and Zanzibar are what overcame the ethnic hatred, religious bigotry, regional parochialism and national differences and forged national cohesion and unity.

It is these that have made Tanzania an example in a continent beset with secessionism, ethnic violence and religious pogroms.

One hopes that there is capacity, honesty and patriotism within Tanzania that will look beyond the sectarian interests.

The alternative is too horrendous to contemplate."

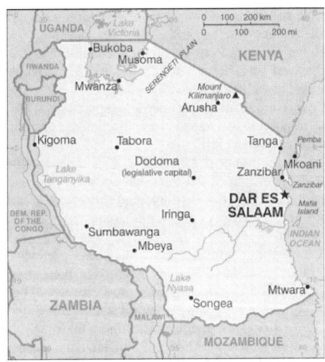

The United Republic of Tanzania

Appendix I:

Reprinted with permission from Godfrey Mwakikagile, *Life in Tanganyika in The Fifties*, Second Edition, Continental Press, 2006, pp. 87 – 140.

Tanganyika
Before Independence

WHAT is Tanzania today did not come into existence until Tanganyika united with Zanzibar in 1964 to form one country.

I was born and brought up in Tanganyika. And it is Tanganyika that I focus on as the land of my birth where my personality and identity was shaped during British colonial rule in the fifties and in the first decade of independence in the sixties.

Tanganyika itself did not exist as a territorial entity until 1885 when it was annexed by Germany. It was created as a colony by the Germans whose claim to the territory was given formal recognition at the Berlin conference during the partition of Africa.

The German Colonization Society led by Dr. Karl Peters claimed the territory in 1884. He was supported by his home government under Bismarck and went on to establish the German East Africa Company to rule the territory.

In 1886 and 1890, the British and the Germans signed agreements which defined their spheres of influence in the interior of East Africa and along the coast previously claimed by the sultan of Oman who had moved his capital from Muscat, Oman, to Zanzibar.

In 1891, the German government took over direct administration of the territory from the German East Africa Company and appointed a governor with headquarters in Dar es Salaam, a port city founded by the Arabs and whose name means Haven of Peace in Arabic.

European powers drew territorial boundaries to define their spheres of influence, creating the countries we have in Africa today.

In East Africa, the British had Kenya, Uganda, and Zanzibar; and the Germans, Tanganyika, and Ruanda-Urundi - what is now Rwanda and Burundi - which together formed one colony called German East Africa which existed from 1885 to 1919.

After that, the British took over what became Tanganyika following Germany's defeat in World War I. The Belgians acquired Ruanda-Urundi which became two separate colonies but administered together with Belgian Congo.

British formal presence on Tanganyikan soil began in 1914 at the beginning of World War I when the Royal Navy occupied Mafia island in the Indian ocean a few miles southeast of Dar es Salaam, the capital.

During World War I, German East Africa was occupied by the Allied forces including troops from South

Africa led by General Smuts. It was - minus Ruanda-Urundi - renamed Tanganyika Territory in 1920 (named after Lake Tanganyika) and placed under the League of Nations mandate administered by Britain after American President Woodrow Wilson refused to assume responsibility for the former German colony as proposed by British Prime Minister Lloyd George of the Liberal Party.

In 1921, the Belgians transferred Kigoma district in western Tanganyika to British administration, making it part of Tanganyika. They had administered the district - together with Ruanda-Urundi - since the Allied occupation of the former German colony in 1916.

And in 1924, Britain and Belgium signed an agreement defining the border between Tanganyika and Ruanda-Urundi.

Until 1925, Tanganyika was administered in an improvised way and followed German administrative practices, after which the system of Indirect Rule was introduced.

Indirect Rule was first practised by Lord Lugard in northern Nigeria where he used traditional rulers including emirs to administer a vast expanse of territory.

In 1946, Tanganyika became a UN trusteeship territory; coincidentally in the same year the Nigerian federation was formed out of three massive regions created by the British: Northern Nigeria dominated by the Hausa-Fulani, Eastern Nigeria by the Igbo, and Western Nigeria by the Yoruba. Nigeria itself was created in 1914 with the amalgamation of the North and the South which had been administered separately as if they were two distinct colonies but under the same colonial power.

When Europeans came to Africa and established colonies, they thought they could transform at least some of those colonies into a permanent home for white settlers as the British did in Australia and New Zealand, as well as in South Africa, Southern Rhodesia - what is Zimbabwe today - and Kenya.

In fact, Kenya was declared a "White Man's Country" from the beginning of formal British occupation of the territory under Lord Delamere.

Delamere owned vast expanses of land in the Rift Valley region of the Kenyan Highlands – called White Highlands during colonial rule – and became the unofficial leader of the white settlers in Kenya.

He was also an active member of the colonial legislature which was known as the Legislative Council of Kenya. And the British settlers were determined to turn the colony into a "white man's country."

Neighbouring Tanganyika would have met the same fate had the British colonialists succeeded in establishing a giant federation stretching from Kenya all the way down to South Africa.

In fact, the governors of all the colonies in the region - Kenya, Uganda, Tanganyika, Nyasaland (now Malawi), Northern Rhodesia (Zambia today), and Southern Rhodesia met in Tukuyu, southern Tanganyika, in 1925 to work on a plan to form such a federation.

But, years later as political awakening among Africans began to take place, the proposed federation was strongly opposed by African nationalists who feared that the establishment of such a giant political entity would consolidate and perpetuate white domination over Africans who constituted the vast majority of the population throughout the region as much as they did in the rest of the continent.

Yet, in spite of such opposition, it is interesting to note that years later Ugandan leader Milton Obote took a firm stand against the dissolution of one federation, the Central African Federation (of Northern Rhodesia, Southern Rhodesia and Nyasaland), an imperial creation, arguing that it would not be in the best interests of Africa if the federation was dissolved.

He argued that it would be beneficial to Africa if the

federation remained intact and became a supra-nation upon attainment of independence.

He was virtually alone among African leaders in his support of the continued existence of the Central African Federation - also known as the Federation of Rhodesia and Nyasaland - which was created in 1953. It was dissolved 10 years later in 1963.

And there were always whites in all these territories who supported Africans in their quest for justice and racial equality across the spectrum, including the former governor of Northern Rhodesia, Sir Roy Welensky, who also once served as federal prime minister of the Federation of Rhodesia and Nyasaland, although his espousal of the doctine of racial equality did not go far enough.

But he at least acknowledged the genuine aspirations of Africans even if he may not have believed that black Africans really deserved the same rights as whites.

Another example, of genuine commitment to racial equality, was Derek Bryceson, a British, who emigrated from Kenya to Tanganyika in 1952 and who became a cabinet member soon after the country won independence.

Then there was Dr. Leader Sterling, also British, who first came to Tanganyika in the 1930s. He also became a nominated member of parliament and a cabinet member appointed by President Julius Nyerere.

Bryceson was also an elected member of parliament representing a predominantly black district, Kilosa, and never lost an election against black political candidates contesting for the same seat; nor did Amir Jamal, of Indian origin, representing Morogoro, who was also, like Bryceson, a cabinet member under Nyerere for more than two decades since independence.

And there were other whites - not only in Tanganyika but in other colonies as well, across the continent - who felt the same way, including those who privately expressed their interest in building multiracial societies on the basis of equality but did not express their feelings publicly for fear of offending and alienating other whites who were not as liberal or open-minded as they were. As Harry Hodson states in his autobiography:

"A new constitution for Southern Rhodesia, which would have kept the white majority in parliament but extended the black franchise, and which had the nucleus of a common electoral roll, had been proposed from London and was being hotly debated. (It was to avert this far from radical constitution that Mr Ian Smith declared UDI two years later.)

Over his customary tankard of beer Sir Edgar Whitehead, the colony's Prime Minister, a taciturn, introspective character, gave me his opinion that if all went according to plan the reforms would give rise to a genuine multiracial government with a multiracial parliament.

Sir Roy Welensky, Prime Minister of the moribund Central African Federation, amid a great deal of bluster, agreed with Whitehead at least on the point that time and opportunity had to be used to break down race barriers.

Sir Robert Tredgold, who later became fainéant head of state under UDI, deplored the lack of communication between Africans and the great majority of Europeans: "the trouble with most of our people here is that they live in a deaf world."

Lord Malvern, who as Sir Godfrey Huggins had been Prime Minister of Southern Rhodesia for 10 years, and at 77 was as amusing, vigorous and earthy as ever, gave a luncheon party for me.

I reminded him that several years earlier, dining with the Round Table Moot, he had likened the mass of Africans in Rhodesia to the London East-Enders among whom he had worked as a young doctor -poor and ignorant, and like children, but as capable as they of education and advance. Did he hold to that? 'Yes - and they will grow up just as quickly.'"

Yet these white Rhodesian leaders were not the most liberal kind. They were racist. For example, Godfrey Huggins, who was acclaimed as a great British liberal, said at a press conference in London in 1952:

"There will be no Africans in a federal government (of Rhodesia - Northern and Southern - and Nyasaland formed in 1953).
They are quite incapable of playing a full part....They may have a university degree, but their background is all wrong.
It is time for the people in England to realize that the white man in Africa is not prepared, and never will be prepared, to accept the African as an equal either socially or politically." - (Godfrey Huggins, quoted by Colin Legum, *The Lonely African*, p. 90).

His racist remarks were published in British papers and elsewhere. I have also quoted him in one of my books, Godfrey Mwakikagile, *Africa and the West*.

But the mere fact that even such racist liberals at one time or another acknowledged the imperative need for change and knew that such change was inevitable; and the more enlightened amongst them articulated genuinely liberal sentiments - that Africans were entitled to racial equality - shows that there were whites who were interested in achieving racial harmony and equality; and a number of them were far more committed to achieving this goal than most of their leaders were.

They could be found in all African countries, including apartheid South Africa. And Tanganyika was no exception.

Therefore the struggle in all these African countries was essentially democratic and not racial - black versus white - best exemplified by the new dispensation in post-apartheid South Africa where common aspirations shared by blacks, whites, Indians, Coloureds and others led to the adoption of one of the most liberal constitutions in the world guaranteeing equality for all South Africans. As one black South African cabinet member said in his emphatic declaration that non-blacks in South Africa were also Africans just like black Africans: "Indians are in India, and Europeans in Europe."

And it's very interesting to know how the European settlers felt about their new life in the colonies they had established under the tropical sun far away from Europe.

In spite of the difficulties they faced living in underdeveloped regions of the world, they were still very much satisfied with their new life. That is why they did not want to leave or return to Europe except in some cases after independence when conditions became intolerable even for many black Africans who were born in those countries.

Political repression and worsening economic conditions became a way of life in many African countries after the end of colonial rule. And through the years, tens of thousands of Africans have left the continent in search of greener pastures especially in the West.

By the end of 2005, there were more than 5 million Africans living outside Africa, tens of thousands of them highly educated and trained professionals. And tens of thousands of African students who go to school in Europe, North America and other parts of the world every year don't return to their home countries or to any other part of Africa after they finish their studies.

At this writing, there were more than 30,000 Nigerian doctors living and working in the United States alone. In New York City, there were more than 600 Ghanaian doctors. In Chicago, there were more doctors from Sierra Leone than there are in Sierra Leone.

And that's just the tip of the iceberg.

About 50,000 Kenyan professionals live and work in

the United States as I write now. That's without even counting those in the United Kingdom where, for historical reasons because of former colonial ties, they have gone to in the past in larger numbers than they have anywhere else.

Add Nigerians, Ghanaians, Tanzanians, Zimbabweans, Zambians, Sierra Leoneans and others who live in Britain, North America and other parts of the world including Australia. Also think about how many Africans from Senegal, the Ivory Coast, Guinea, Mali and other former French African colonies live and work in France alone. And why.

Then you can see why our continent is in such a mess. It is a continental crisis, a massive brain drain, and it is killing Africa because of rotten leadership - more than anything else - in most parts of the continent since the end of colonial rule.

And we have to be brutally frank about it. Glossing over the problem is not going to solve it.

Those are grim statistics. They tell a sad story about the conditions in our countries which force tens of thousands of highly educated people including professionals such as doctors, engineers, scientists and many others in different critical fields to flee the continent every year in search of better life in Western countries and elsewhere in the industrialized world. They constitute the critical mass without which Africa cannot develop. They keep on fleeing the continent. And it has been that way since independence.

In fact many Africans, especially the older ones, remember with nostalgia how life was in "the good ol' days" before independence when there was law and order and no shortages of essential items. They also remember that they could get jobs, even if the jobs weren't paying much; and that in spite of difficulties, roads and railways were well-maintained, and the people could travel to different parts of the country without fear of being robbed or killed.

And they did not have to pay bribes in those days to get a job, buy a bus ticket or even a simple bar of soap or some toothpaste as happened in many countries across the continent after independence.

Those are some of the reasons why many people remember the fifties with nostalgia; a nostalgic feeling which may seem to justify or defend colonial rule although that is not the case. It is simply a desire by many people to live better, even if simpler, lives. And the deplorable condition in which tens of millions of Africans live more than 40 years after independence is a searing indictment against Africa's post-colonial leadership.

It is no wonder that millions of Africans who are old enough to have lived under colonial rule remember those days with nostalgia.

For whites, life was even better for them when compared with the way Africans lived. In fact, life couldn't have been better for some of them since many colonial administrators would not have been able to get in their own countries - in Britain and elsewhere in Europe - the kind of jobs they had in colonial Africa.

Since I focus on Tanganyika in this chapter, the examples I cite come from East Africa to illustrate my point. As Erika Johnson, writing about the 1950s in colonial Tanganyika, stated in *The Other Side of Kilimanjaro*:

"Robin [Robin Johnson was a District Commissioner, simply known as D.C. throughout British colonial Africa] maintains that there was no better life for a man in those days than that of a District Commissioner. It was a marvellous combination of an active open air life, coupled with a wide, varied and interesting amount of office work.

You did long walking safaris through your area and slept under canvas, and in this way you got to know your parishioners and their problems.

162

Responsible for a vast area, you were father, mentor and disciplinarian to everyone, sorting out family and tribal disputes. You had to do anything and everything: build roads, dams and bridges, dig wells and be a magistrate and administrator of law and order.

Your problems could vary from shooting a rogue elephant despoiling villagers' crops to trying a stock thief in court.

In later years, [Julius] Nyerere once said to a silent Robin that the D.C's had made little contribution other than collecting taxes!"

Many of those projects provided employment for a number of Africans. And they played a major role in building roads, dams and bridges, making bricks, digging wells and doing many other things, providing cheap labour.

In fact, I personally remember seeing African men doing hard work, building roads, in the town and on the outskirts of Mbeya and also working on the road from Mbeya to Chunya, a district north of Mbeya; and in Rungwe district working on the road from Tukuyu to Kyela, 30 miles south of Tukuyu close to the Tanganyika-Nyasaland (now Malawi) border, when I was a little boy under 10 in the 1950s.

They worked for the colonial Public Works Department, what was simply known as PWD, and rode in the back of Bedford lorries; they were British lorries imported from Britain. The lorries also were simply called PWD. I even remember their colour. They were painted green on the sides and white on top.

The African labourers worked hard, all day long, often in scorching sun.

The buses which used those roads, besides other vehicles, were the East African Railways & Harbours Corporation (EAR&H) buses. I remember they were Leyland buses.

163

The wages for Africans working on those roads and elsewhere were low but better than nothing if you needed some money to buy a few things now and then.

Many other Africans earned some money by selling agricultural products, and sometimes handicrafts, at open markets in villages and sometimes in town. In our case it was in the town of Tukuyu, built on small hills with a majestic view below and all the way down to Lake Nyasa clearly visible about 34 miles away on the Malawi-Tanzania border.

Some of the people at the market whom I remember vividly were Kikuyu women. They were originally from Kenya and had, like many other Kenyans, come to Tanganyika to take advantage of the opportunities available to make money in a country where the indigenous people, including my fellow Nyakyusa in Rungwe District, were supposedly not as aggressive as the Kenyans were.

The Kenyans were seen as "more enterprising," "more adventurous," "more aggressive" and "more of risk-takers" than Tanganyikans; although all those are relative terms.

Even today, many Tanzanians are apprehensive about their future in the proposed East African Federation which is supposed to be consummated by 2013 or even later, if at all. They say the federation will be dominated by Kenyans and Ugandans who are more "aggressive" and better educated.

They also say problems of tribalism and racism, so common in Kenya, Uganda and in Rwanda and Burundi unlike in Tanzania, will spread to Tanzania and the country will lose the peace and stability it has enjoyed since independence.

When I recall the fifties and early sixties, I can understand why many of my fellow countrymen feel the way they do in terms of competition between Tanzanians and Kenyans as well as Ugandans in the economic arena, besides their fear of tribalism and racism becoming major problems in Tanzania - which will be no more - if the countries do indeed unite to form a supra-nation.

I remember what my mother said more than once in the late fifties and early sixties after she saw Kikuyu women at the market in Tukuyu when she now and then went into town to but a variety of items. She described them as very aggressive and determined to make money. They were the first to arrive at the market early in the morning before dawn to make sure that they had the best spots where they could attract the largest number of customers.

I went to the market myself a few times and I remember seeing them selling beans, rice and other items.

And what was so good about all this is that there was no hostility towards the Kikuyu on the part of the Nyakyusa.

I don't remember hearing anyone saying these Kikuyus have come all the way from Kenya to Rungwe District, down here, near the border with Nyasaland and Northern Rhodesia to take over our market and steal our customers! It was business as usual, although many Nyakyusas were outmaneuvred on their own turf, at their own market, in their own town and home district, by these "strangers" from Kenya.

But some of them may have learnt a thing or two from these Kikuyu women who had mastered the art of salesmanship and tricks of the trade. However, most of the Nyakyusa women at the market were equally competent and were a perfect match for the Kikuyu and may even have welcomed the challenge from them to demonstrate their own marketing skills. The challenge itself was a source of inspiration to others to excel and was therefore a positive thing.

Besides the women and some men selling food and other items at the market in Tukuyu, there were other Africans - although not many - who worked in that town. My father was one of them. He was assistant manager at a

Shell BP petrol station under a British manager. I remember the manager had a son who was around my age. Whenever I went to see my father now and then when I was in town for a walk or to buy a few things, I would see the boy there with his father.

It has been more than 40 years since I last bought some items from the Indian shops in the town of Tukuyu - they were the only ones, except one Somali shop owned by Rajab who knew my father well - but I still remember some of the owners and the names of those shops, Hirji, Merali, and Makanji which were also said to be the biggest in town. There were no African shops in Tukuyu in those days.

I remember that some Indian shop owners even spoke Kinyakyusa, the native language of the Nyakyusa in Rungwe District, and they had good relations with their customers. I also remember seeing and listening to many Nyakyusa women negotiating with the shop owners over price when they were buying clothes, sugar, cooking oil, kerosene for their lamps in the villages and other items.

One of the popular items bought by some women was a cotton cloth called *mwasungo* in Kinyakyusa. It was black and cheap and the people who bought that were usually very poor. If you bought *mwasungo*, people would assume you had nothin'. Some people even made fun of the material. It's sad but it happened.

Hardly any African women worked in the town of Tukuyu except may be a *yaya* (house maid) here and there.

There were, however, a few men who worked as watchmen staying awake all night long outside Indian shops with their *pangas*, in spite of the fact that we never heard of anybody trying to break into the shops - which were also Indian family residences - even when there were no night watchmen at all at some of the shops.

My father was one of the few men who had a regular job in Tukuyu when he worked as an assistant manager at the Shell BP petrol station.

I also remember one very small African restaurant near the football field in the town of Tukuyu. The soccer field was also used by politicians to address mass rallies.

I remember my father took me to that restaurant quite often when we were in town and he knew the owners well.

But it was Africans working on road projects, building or repairing roads, who were probably the most visible people in the labour market of the formal sector besides teachers and other employees.

I saw them working on roads many times in the fifties. And I remember many of them liked to sing or shout a lot when they worked, repairing or building roads. They worked hard until late in the evening, sometimes until dusk.

During those days of colonial rule, Tanganyika was divided into seven provinces:

The Southern Highlands Province, the Southern Province, the Central Province, the Western Province, the Lake Province, the Coast Province, and the Northern Province. After independence, the Southern Highlands was divided into Mbeya Region and Iringa Region; so were the rest, also broken down into smaller regional administrative units called Regions.

I also remember that the fifties were a period when many people from Tanganyika went to work in the mines in South Africa. Some of them came from my area of Kyimbila which has several villages including Mpumbuli, my home village, about four miles – south – from the town of Tukuyu. One of the people who went to work in the mines in South Africa was my cousin Daudi who lived in a different part of Rungwe District several miles away from Kyimbila.

Coincidentally, Daudi's father William, my father's elder brother, migrated to South Africa in the mid- or late forties never to be heard from again, except once or twice when he wrote my father back then not long after he

167

settled in South Africa. Until this day, we don't know what happened to him or if he got married again and had another family in South Africa. If he did, we will probably never know about that.

Although I was under 10 years old in the fifties, I remember that the people who went to work in the mines were flown from Mbeya to South Africa. I remember talking to some of those who came back, including my cousin Daudi, and asking them about South Africa.

They had plenty of stories to tell about the City of Gold and how big it was. They also told us stories about the fights they had in the mines with people of other ethnic groups. The Nyakyusa, the people of my ethnic group, had a reputation on the mine compounds as fierce fighters.

The fifties were without question some of the most important years of my life. They were my formative years as much as the sixties were.

And I remember listening to many inspiring stories which helped to enlarge my mental horizon at such an early age. And they have remained a source of inspiration throughout my life. My father was one of the people who liked to tell stories about hard work and success in life and played a critical role in shaping my personality when I was growing up.

I also remember hearing stories of valour about the Nyakyusa during my time and in the past including their successful campaigns against the Ngoni in the 1830s, '40s and '50s when the Ngoni tried to invade and penetrate Nyakyusaland. The Nyakyusa also successfully repelled the Sangu who invaded our district in the 1870s and 1880s from neighbouring Usangu in Mbeya District. Like the Nyakyusa, the Sangu had a quite a reputation as fierce fighters. But they were no match for the Nyakyusa who stopped their incursions into Nyakyusaland.

The few white missionaries who settled in Rungwe District also tried to intervene and act as mediators in the conflicts not only between the Nyakyusa and the Sangu but also between the Nyakyusa and the Safwa, then the largest ethnic group in Mbeya District until they were later outnumbered by the Nyakyusa. They also played a mediating role in other conflicts including intra-tribal (or intra-ethnic) disputes but not always successfully.

But, besides the Nyakyusa, it was the Ngoni whom I remember the most for their reputation as fighters mainly because I interacted with them in the sixties. Their legendary reputation as fighters sent a chill down the spine and many of their neighbours were afraid of them, except a few like the Nyakyusa, and the Hehe who, under their leader Chief Mkwawa, once defeated the Germans.

Originally from Natal Province in South Africa, the Ngoni settled in Songea District in southern Tanganyika, as well as in Sumbawanga in the western part of the country where they came to be known as the Fipa, which is their ethnic name and identity even today. They had a reputation as fierce fighters even in South Africa itself before they left during the *imfecane* in the 1820s and '30s headed north, finally settling in what is now Malawi, Mozambique and Tanzania. Some of them even went to Congo after going through Tanganyika.

I went to Songea Secondary School which was a boarding school in Songea District, the home district of the Ngoni, in southern Tanzania and talked to many Ngonis including some who were old enough to be my parents when I was in my teens back then in the sixties. Almost without exception, they all recalled the stories they were told by their elders when they were growing up on how the Nyakyusa and the Ngoni fought when the Ngoni tried to invade and conquer Nyakyusaland, to no avail.

They told me that the Nyakyusa *ni watani wetu*, a Swahili expression meaning they are our friends and we tell jokes about each other. Many of those "jokes" have to do with how hard the Nyakyusa fought to repel the Ngoni invaders after the Ngoni failed to steal Nyakyusa cows and women!

Some of the Ngoni also went to work in the mines in South Africa - where they originally came from - but not in significant numbers as the Nyakyusa and other people from the Southern Highlands did, especially from Rungwe and Mbeya Districts in a region bordering what was then Northern Rhodesia, now Zambia.

Northern Rhodesia itself attracted many mine workers from my region and many of them settled in that country. Even today, you will find many Nyakyusas who settled in Kitwe and other parts of the Copperbelt many years ago after they went to work there in the mines. For example, in 1954 the Nyakyusa in Kitwe formed an organisation to preserve, protect and promote their interests as a collective entity.

The Lozi, members of another ethnic group from Baraotseland or Barotse Province and one of the largest in Zambia, also formed their own organisation around the same time, as did others and some even before then including the Ngoni. And they were all cited as examples of ethnic solidarity among the mine workers in Kitwe and other parts of the Copperbelt in Northern Rhodesia. The Nyakyusa presence in what is now Zambia is still strong even today.

In fact, one of my mother's first cousins who was older than my mother emigrated from Tanganyika to Northern Rhodesia as a young man in the early 1940s. He was the son of my mother's uncle Asegelile Mwankemwa who was the pastor of our church, Kyimbila Moravian Church at Kyimbila in Rungwe District. He also lived in South Africa for a number of years before returning to Northern Rhodesia where he eventually became a high government official after the country won independence as Zambia.

He returned to Tanzania in the 1990s to spend his last days in the land of his birth. Tragically, he had forgotten Kinyakyusa and did not know Kiswahili after so many years of absence from Tanganyika, later Tanzania, and could communicate only in English and Bemba, one of the

170

major languages in Zambia. All his children were also born and brought up in Northern Rhodesia.

And he was just one of the many people from my district who migrated to Northern Rhodesia and even some of them to South Africa. Jobs in the mines in both countries was the biggest attraction, encouraging many Tanganyikans to go there in those days.

The town of Mbeya was their main departure point heading south and was the largest town in the region. It was also the capital of the Southern Highlands Province when I was growing up.

The people who had been recruited to work in the mines in South Africa boarded planes called WENELA. I remember that name very well because I heard it all the time when I was growing up in the fifties. The people would say so-and-so has gone to Wenela, meaning to work in the mines in South Africa. The term became an integral part of our vocabulary in the 1950s, probably as much as it was even before then among the Nyakyusa and others.

The name WENELA was an acronym for the Witwatersrand Native Labour Association which was responsible for the recruitment of cheap labour among Africans in neighbouring countries including Tanganyika to work in the mines in South Africa. They were sometimes recruited to work in other sectors of the economy but primarily in the mines.

Many of the people who were recruited in Tanganyika were flown down there unlike, for example, those from Basutoland (now Lesotho) or Bechuanaland (now Botswana) who, because of their proximity to South Africa, were transported by buses.

But many people from Tanganyika were also transported by road from Mbeya in the Southern Highlands to Broken Hill in Northern Rhodesia. And from there they were taken to Mungu in Barotseland, the western province of Northern Rhodesia, and then flown to Francistown in Bechuanaland; and finally transported by railway to Johannesburg.

Working in the mines was hard labour, with little pay. But it was still something for people who virtually had nothing in terms of money. That's why they were drawn down there.

I remember my cousin Daudi worked for three years in the mines in Johannesburg. But when he came back to Tanganyika, he hardly had anything besides a wooden box he used as a "suitcase" - and which was the only popular and common "suitcase" among many Africans in those days - and may be a couple of shirts, two pairs of trousers, and a simple pair of shoes he wore when he returned home. In fact, he came straight to our village, from Johannesburg, to live with us.

My father was also his father, and the only one had, since his own biological father migrated to South Africa. His father left behind two children, Daudi himself, and his only sister, Esther, who was also younger than Daudi. Tragically, she died only a few years after Daudi returned from South Africa.

He went to South Africa to earn some money, yet returned hardly with any. It was hard life not only for him but for most Africans who went to work in the mines and even for those who remained in the villages.

In general the people were not starving in Tanganyika in the fifties. There was plenty of food especially in fertile regions such as the Southern Highlands where I come from. And my home district of Rungwe is one of the most fertile in the entire East Africa and on the whole continent. Almost anything, any kind of food, grows there: from bananas to sweet potatoes, groundnuts to beans, and all kinds of fruits and vegetables, besides cash crops such as coffee and tea, and much more.

But the people were poor in terms of financial resources. They had very little money. And that is why some of them went all the way to South Africa and to neighbouring Northern Rhodesia to work in the mines.

Some of them also ended up in Katanga Province, in the Congo, which is about 300 miles west from my home region of Mbeya. With all its minerals as the treasure trove of Congo, Katanga Province was another prime destination for job seekers from neighbouring countries who were looking for jobs in the mines.

The Nyakyusa from my home district were some of the people who ended up there. For example, I vividly remember a photograph of a Nyakyusa family published in the *Daily News*, Dar es Salaam, when I worked there as a news reporter in the early seventies.

They had lived in Congo for about 40 years but were expelled from the country and forced to return to Tanzania in what seemed to be a xenophobic campaign fuelled by anti-foreign sentiments in spite of the fact that members of this family, as well as many others, had lived in Congo for decades and their children were born and brought up there.

Therefore there was quite a contrast in terms of living standards between Africans and Europeans as well as between Africans and Asians; also between Africans and Arabs. Africans were the poorest.

But there was no hostility, at least not overt, on the part of Africans towards whites and others in spite of such disparity in living standards; not to the extent that the social order was threatened in a way that could have led to chaos in the country.

For me as a child growing up, life was good as much as it was for many other youngsters. Our parents took care of us. I was never hungry. I always had clothes, although not shoes all the time. My father even gave me pocket money to buy sweets, soft drinks such as Fanta, Sprite and Coca Cola; cake and other delicacies as well as other things I wanted to buy including marbles we boys used to play a game called *goroli* in Kiswahili. It was one of my favourite games.

And for the colonial rulers as well as other whites, life was much better than ours in many respects. They usually had a lot more money than we did; and they had many things we didn't have.

There are also some things I remember about the kind of relationship some of us had with them as children.

There is one thing in particular which always comes to mind when I recall those days as a young boy in Rungwe District in the 1950s and how I saw whites.

I remember British men and women playing golf and tennis in Tukuyu, the administrative capital of Rungwe district, four miles from our home village and about 30 miles from the Tanzania-Malawi border.

Many of them were friendly and they used to give us tennis balls now and then when we passed through the golf course. Quite a few of them came from as far away as Mbeya, the provincial capital, 45 miles north of Tukuyu, and some even from neighboring Northern Rhodesia, now Zambia.

I was, of course, too young then to know what was going on in terms of colonial domination, or what it meant to be ruled by the British or Europeans in general.

But I do remember that whenever we saw them, they seemed to be very happy and satisfied with their lives, which were made much easier by African servants in almost every European household. It was unthinkable not to have one, since they all could afford it. African servants provided cheap labour.

But Africans also needed the money and they were glad to have jobs as house maids and as house boys or as farm workers working for Europeans. They also, the men especially, had to have a way to earn some money in order to pay taxes. Otherwise they would be in serious trouble with the colonial authorities. And like in every other country, there were those who simply did not want to pay taxes even if you told them, and could prove to them, that the money would be used to help them as well.

Europeans were in full control and the colonial authorities had no interest in sharing power with Africans,

Asians or Arabs on equal basis as equal citizens of the same country. Yet there were whites who worked with Africans and other non-whites for the benefit of all. Therefore it would be a mistake to say that there were no whites in Tanganyika or in other parts of Africa who were interested in the well-being of Africans.

In fact, many of them were Africans themselves as citizens of African countries. Or they considered themselves to be Africans because they were born and brought up in Africa even if they retained British citizenship or that of any other European country. And when some of them had to leave for different reasons, they were sad they had to go, leaving a country or countries they knew as their home.

In spite of all that, there are still millions of white Africans in Africa, mostly in South Africa, about five million of them. And there are tens of thousands of others elsewhere in different countries on the continent. Their identity as Africans and allegiance to Africa inspired coinage of the term "white tribes" of Africa.

But there were some who were die-hard colonialists and had no intention of sharing power or identifying with non-whites - black Africans, Asians and Arabs - as fellow Africans. They were the ones who were opposed to independence in spite of the fact that there were whites who supported the nationalist aspirations of the Africans in their quest for independence or simply acknowledged the fact that independence would come some day whether they liked it or not.

Some British settlers formed the United Tanganyika Party, known as UTP, to stem the nationalist tide that started to sweep across the country. But in spite of the differences they had with those who felt that Tanganyika should be a truly multiracial society ruled on democratic basis, there was no bitterness or hostility between the two sides which characterized race relations in some parts of Africa.

Leaders such as Julius Nyerere, Derek Bryceson, Amir H. Jamal who was of Indian descent, Dr. Leader Sterling and their colleagues argued that the future of Tanganyika as a nation and as a united country could not be guaranteed without racial equality.

And when some African members of TANU argued that people of other races should not be allowed to join the party or become citizens of Tanganyika after the country won independence, Nyerere made it clear that he would resign as a leader; a threat which brought others back in line to conform to the wishes of the majority of the TANU members who were committed to the creation of a truly non-racial society in which no one would be denied equal rights as explained by Nyerere and others during the campaign for independence.

Unlike West Africa, East Africa attracted a large number of white settlers for different reasons. One of the main reasons was climate. Another one was the fact that the largest number of British colonies in Africa were in East, Central and southern Africa; which partly explains why a significant number of British settlers ended up in that part of the continent.

The largest number of the white settlers in Tanganyika and other parts of East Africa were not colonial administrators or rulers but ordinary citizens who simply wanted to live in Africa. Others went there because they had been offered jobs. Yet others felt that there was great potential for employment and economic development in different fields in those countries.

One of the areas in which British settlers in East Africa became deeply involved was commercial farming. East Africa is endowed with an abundance of fertile land, much of it at high altitude with a cooler climate, although still tropical. But it somewhat reminded the Europeans of the temperate climate back home in Europe, at temperatures they were comfortable with, and many of them came to settle in this region.

Much of East Africa is, of course, also hot, in fact very hot; for example along the coast, in the lowlands and in other parts of the region. But it also has more arable land, at higher altitudes, than West Africa does. For example, in an area where I come from called Kyimbila, there is a large tea estate called Kyimbila Tea Estate stretching for miles; we also grow a lot of coffee in our district.

The area of Kyimbila, including my home village of Mpumbuli, also has many pine trees. We even have some on our family property. These are the kind of trees which grow in temperate zones or in a cool climate.

Kyimbila Tea Estate is one of the largest tea estates in Tanzania, indeed in the whole of East Africa, and was originally established by the Germans. In fact, there was a German settlement at Kyimbila, about a mile and a half from our house, when the Germans ruled Tanganyika as *Deutsch Ostafrika* (German East Africa), and built a large church there, called Kyimbila Moravian Church.

There is also a large grave yard at Kyimbila where Germans are buried; I remember reading the headstones showing the deceased were born in the 1800s; they were born in Germany. After the Germans lost World War I, the British took over the tea estate.

When the British ran the tea estate when I was growing up, they always had a British manager who lived on the premises. And as a child, I did not know what colonial rule meant. But I knew that living conditions for white people were better than ours. And I still remember quite a few incidents in those years.

One incident I vividly remember had to do with my father when he worked as an assistant manager at a Shell BP station in the town of Tukuyu about four miles from our home in Mpumbuli village. He sometimes used to take lunch to work and one day he was told by the British manager of the petrol station that he could not put his lunch on the table used by the manager; it was *chapati* my mother had cooked for him on that day. I remember that

177

very well.

My father was very bitter about the incident and told us what happened when he came back home that evening. That was around 1958 or 1959. My father, having secondary school education, was one of the few people in the area who knew English. And that was one of the reasons why he was hired as the assistant manager at the petrol station. He went to Malangali Secondary School in Iringa district in the Southern Highlands Province, one of the best schools in colonial Tanganyika and even after independence.

Before going back to Tukuyu, he worked as a medical assistant in many parts of Tanganyika - in Muheza, Tanga, Handeni, Amani, Kilosa, Morogoro - including the town of Kigoma, in western Tanganyika, where I was born.

He was trained as a medical assistant in the mid-1940s at Muhimbili National Hospital (then known as Sewa Haji and later Princess Margaret Hospital) in Dar es Salaam during British colonial rule.

He excelled in school and was supposed to go to Tabora Secondary School for further education in standard 11 and standard 12 after completing standard 10 at Malangali Secondary School but couldn't go further because of family obligations, forcing him to seek employment early.

One of his classmates at Muhimbili National Hospital was Austin Shaba who, after completing his studies, went to Tukuyu to work as a medical assistant, and later became minister of local government in the first independence cabinet under President Nyerere. I remember my father saying Austin - they knew each other well - encouraged him to go into politics but he refused to do so.

Another classmate of my father at Malangali Secondary School who also went into politics was Jeremiah Kasambala. The son of a chief, he also became a cabinet member under President Nyerere and served as minister of agriculture and cooperatives in the first

178

independence cabinet.

He came from the area of Mpuguso where I attended middle school in Rungwe District. He and my father had known each other for years and he equally encouraged him to pursue a career in politics. But, again, my father refused to do so although he was interested in politics and kept up with what was going on in Tanganyika and elsewhere.

He listened to the BBC in English and Kiswahili everyday and had a profound influence on me. I also started listening to the BBC at a very young age in the fifties when I was under ten years old.

I did not know English then, so I listened to the Swahili Service on the BBC and on TBC (Tanganyika Broadcasting Corporation) broadcast from Dar es Salaam more than 300 miles away.

And to make sure that I was paying attention, my father would sometimes walk away from the radio and then ask me later to give him a summary of the news. I already had a good memory and this exercise only helped improve it further.

I also remember the kind of shortwave radio we had. It was Philips, with an external antennae stretched out and attached to a pole, sometimes a dry bamboo tree, outside the house. All this reminds of the simpler life many people had in Tanganyika in the fifties. It had its inconveniences, and quite a few of them for Africans because of poverty, but still exciting.

It was also during the fifties that the campaign for independence in Tanganyika began in earnest. Like in most parts of Africa, it was a non-violent campaign unlike in neighbouring Kenya where it became violent during Mau Mau. Although I was very young when Mau Mau was going on, I remember seeing pictures of Mau Mau fighters in some newspapers published in Kiswahili. The most vivid image I still have of these fighters was their hair style, what they call dreadlocks nowadays.

The main Kiswahili papers during those days were

Mambo Leo and *Mwafrika.* And I remember others: *Ngurumo, Mwangaza* and *Baragumu.* Although *Baragumu* was published in Kiswahili, it was not sympathetic to the nationalist cause articulated by TANU during the struggle for independence. It was, instead, used by the United Tanganyika Party (UTP) to promote its agenda among Africans by telling them that the country was not ready for independence and that supporting TANU would not serve their interests.

UTP was founded in February 1956 with the encouragement of Governor Sir Edward Twining as a counterweight to TANU in order to maintain the privileged status of the white minority settlers and was one of the three main political parties in Tanganyika before independence. It supported a multi-racial constitution but rejected universal suffrage without which genuine democratic representation is impossible.

The other party was the radical African National Congress (ANC) formed by Zuberi Mtemvu in 1958. Mtemvu and his supporters broke away from TANU because they were highly critical of Nyerere's moderate policies advocating equality for all Tanganyikans regardless of race.

The ANC argued that the interests of Africans were paramount even if it meant sacrificing the interests and well-being of whites, Asians and Arabs. Nyerere was resolutely opposed to that and won overwhelming support from the vast majority of the people in Tanganyika for his policies of racial tolerance and equality.

One of the organs he used to articulate his views was a Kiswahili newspaper, *Sauti Ya TANU* (Voice of TANU) founded in 1957. He edited the paper himself.

The main English newspaper was the Tanganyika *Standard*, the oldest English newspaper in the country founded in 1930. And it had a lot to do with my life only a few years later.

The future was never meant for us to see, and had

someone told me back then in the late 1950s that my life would somehow be influenced by that English newspaper, I would not have believed it even at such a tender age.

But that is exactly what happened. About 10 years later, I joined the editorial staff of the *Standard* in Dar es Salaam. I was first hired as a new reporter in June 1969 when I was still a student at Tambaza High School, formerly H.H. The Aga Khan, in Dar es Salaam. I was 19 years old and the youngest reporter on the staff. I was hired by David Martin, the news editor, and Brendon Grimshaw, the managing editor.

After completing Form VI, I joined the National Service which was mandatory for all those who finished secondary school and high school. After National Service, I worked briefly at the Ministry of Information and Broadcasting in Dar es Salaam as an information officer before returning to the *Standard* which was renamed the *Daily News* after it was nationalized in 1970.

And in November 1972, my editor Benjamin Mkapa, whom we simply called Ben Mkapa, helped me to go to school in the United States for further education. My trip was financed by the newspaper. They bought me a plane ticket and gave me a travelling allowance.

Years later, Mkapa was elected president of Tanzania and served two five-year terms.

Had I not joined the *Standard* as a news reporter, I may not have gone to school in the United States. And you probably would not be reading this book or any of the others I have written.

Although the *Standard* was a colonial newspaper in the fifties and articulated the sentiments of the white settler community and defended colonial policies, it provided ample coverage of political events during the struggle for independence even if such coverage was not always balanced and quite often reflected official thinking of the colonial authorities.

I remember when I was a news reporter at the *Standard*

before it was nationalized in 1970, our rivals at the militant newspaper, *The Nationalist* which was the official organ of the ruling party TANU, used to publish stories, editorials and feature articles in which they said we worked for "an imperialist newspaper" and sometimes even called us "imperialist agents"!

We simply ignored them, and even laughed at them, whenever we came face-to-face covering the same events. There was no hostility between us. They were simply articulating the ideological position of the ruling party which owned the paper they worked for.

And many of them believed that, because of their ideological zealotry.

And although the *Standard* defended white minority interests during colonial rule, it did not ignore what was going on in those days, even if it wanted to, and the leading African nationalist during that time, Julius Nyerere, had his views published in the paper many times, although not always the way he had articulated them. There was usually a slant in favour of the colonial government, since the paper was its organ even if not officially so.

And as a moderate who was also committed to building a multiracial society, Nyerere was seen as a responsible leader who was not a threat to the interests of racial minorities in the country. He also sought to achieve his goals by constitutional means. Therefore ignoring him, or refusing to report what he said at public rallies and in interviews would have been counterproductive and not in the best interests of the white settlers.

Although Nyerere was committed to non-violence to achieve independence, he could not guarantee that some of the people in Tanganyika would not resort to violence as some, especially the Kikuyu, did in neighbouring Kenya. As Robert A. Senser, an American journalist and editor of *Human Rights for Workers*, recalled what Nyerere told him when they met in the United States in 1957 in his article, "Remembering A Visitor from Tanganyika," published in *Human Rights for Workers: Bulletin No. IV-22*, December 1, 1999, not long after Nyerere died:

"The other day Ed Marciniak, once a Chicago colleague of mine in editing a monthly called *Work*, mailed me the obituary of Julius Nyerere, president of Tanzania from 1964 to 1985.

Stapled to the clipping was a note from Ed saying: 'I still remember your interview with him in *Work*.'

After all these years, I also remember that interview one evening 42 years ago, when Nyerere had dinner with my wife and me in our small apartment on Chicago's South Side.

Nyerere, 35, then president of a political party in a British colony in East Africa called Tanganyika, had just come from London, where the British colonial secretary had rejected his case for Britain loosening its hold on the colony.

'It's a tragic state of affairs,' Nyerere told me, 'because the British government has an attitude that in effect says, 'There's no trouble in Tanganyika--no Mau Mau there or anything of that sort. So why bother with it?"

That quotation is from a yellowed clipping in an old scrapbook of mine--a page one article in the January 1957 issue of *Work*.

Its headline, based on Nyerere's prediction, was: 'Africa: Free in 30 Years.'

As I wrote my article, Nyerere quickly added that the prediction 'sounds absurd to many, especially to the white settlers in Tanganyika.'

History Can Outpace Human Expectations

In fact, of course, freedom came much quicker than even Nyerere expected. In 1962, only five years after we spoke, Nyerere, head of the Tanganyika African National

Union, became Prime Minister of the newly independent Tanganyika and then, three years later, after his country's union with nearby Zanzibar, President of the new state of Tanzania. He retired voluntarily in 1985.

In the article I mentioned Nyerere's early career as a teacher in a Catholic secondary school in Dar es Salaam, the capital, before he started devoting full time to politics. The obituary, from the *London Tablet*, emphasizes that throughout his adult life Nyerere 'never ceased to be a teacher by temperament, mission, and title: he was always Mwalimu.'

After citing his political successes and failures, and his many talents (he translated two Shakespeare plays into Swahili), the article concludes with this tribute:

'It is, nevertheless, Nyerere's moral example which made him so exceptional, the image of a President standing patiently in a queue waiting to make his confession at the cathedral in Dar: a humble, intellectually open and ascetic teacher, the true Mwalimu.

Unlike almost all the other successful political leaders of his generation in Africa, he was uncorrupted either by power or wealth....Gentle, humorous, radical, persistent, he remained the icon of a truly ecumenical Christian approach to politics and human development.'"

Although Tanganyika won independence and was therefore no longer under British colonial rule, not everything changed overnight.

There were some whites who did not accept the change and refused to treat black Africans and other non-whites as equals even in public places. They were a minority but they did exist.

Andrew Nyerere, the eldest son of President Julius Nyerere and my schoolmate at Tambaza High School in Dar es Salaam from 1969 to 1970, told me about one such incident when I was writing a book, *Nyerere and Africa: End of an Era: Expanded Edition*, after I contacted him to

184

find out if he had something to say that I could add to the book. As he stated in his letter in 2003:

"As you remember, Sheikh Amri Abeid was the first mayor of Dar es Salaam. Soon after independence, the mayor went to Palm Beach Hotel (near our high school, Tambaza, in Upanga).

There was a sign at the hotel which clearly stated: 'No Africans and dogs allowed inside.' He was blocked from entering the hotel, and said in protest, 'But I am the Mayor.' Still he was told, 'You will not get in.'

Shortly thereafter, the owner of the hotel was given 48 hours to leave the country. When the nationalization exercise began (in 1967), that hotel was the first to be nationalized."

But in spite of such incidents, and they were rare, race relations were good in general, in fact very good sometimes, as they were before independence.

For the vast majority of Tanganyikans of all races, including non-citizens, life in general went on as before as if no major political changes had taken place in the country ending colonial rule.

Even during the struggle for independence indignities of colour bar experienced by Africans now and then, here and there, did not fuel animosity towards whites among Africans to make them rebellious.

There was potential for revolt just like in any situation, anywhere, when people are demanding basic human rights and those demands are not met.

But in the case of Tanganyika, conditions were no close to what they were in apartheid South Africa; nor was land alienation as serious or widespread as it was in Kenya, especially in the Central Province where the Kikuyu revolted against the British.

There were, however, incidents in Tanganyika which clearly showed that fundamental change was needed if the different races were to live in harmony.

Nyerere himself was involved in one such incident in the fifties (and there were others) just before he formally began to campaign for independence; he was already, even by then, the most prominent African leader in Tanganyika as president of the Tanganyika African Association (TAA) which was transformed into TANU in 1954. As Colin Legum, a South African of British descent who knew and interviewed many African leaders including Nyerere and Nkrumah, stated in a chapter, "The Goal of an Egalitarian Soceity," he contributed to a book, *Mwalimu: The Influence of Nyerere*:

"I was privileged to meet Nyerere while he was still a young teacher in short trousers at the very beginning of his political career, and to engage in private conversations with him since the early 1950s.

My very first encounter in 1953 taught me something about his calm authority in the face of racism in colonial Tanganyika.

I had arranged a meeting with four leaders of the nascent nationalist movement at the Old Africa Hotel in Dar es Salaam. We sat at a table on the pavement and ordered five beers, but before we could lift our glasses an African waiter rushed up and whipped away all the glasses except mine.

I rose to protest to the white manager, but Nyerere restrained me. 'I'm glad it happened,' he said, ' now you can go and tell your friend Sir Edward Twining [the governor at the time] how things are in this country.'

His manner was light and amusing, with no hint of anger."

This incident demonstrates one simple truth about Tanganyika in the fifties and throughout the entire colonial period under British rule.

It was not a rigidly segregated society; and whatever

racial separation existed was in most cases voluntary and not strictly enforced even by convention.

There were no laws against racial integration. Had there been such laws, Colin Legum would not even have thought about going to the white manager to protest against what happened to his African colleagues whose glasses of beer were taken away by an African waiter at the Old Africa Hotel in Dar es Salaam.

Had this been apartheid South Africa, or had Tanganyika been a segregated society in the legal sense, separating the races, Nyerere and other Africans who were with him on that day would not have entered the Old Africa Hotel without being arrested. And their sympathetic friend, Colin Legum, who had invited them, would have been arrested as well, not only for defying convention but for breaking the law.

But the incident also showed that without fundamental change in the system, there would be trouble in the country even with Nyerere as the leader of those campaigning for independence.

After independence, Nyerere remained restrained in the conduct of national affairs and earned a reputation as a tolerant leader. But he also had a reputation of being tough and uncompromising on matters of principle especially involving equality.

One of his major achievements was containing and neutralizing radical elements in the ruling party who wanted to marginalize racial minorities in national life, forcing them to live on the periphery of the mainstream.

There were even those who would have resorted to outright expulsion of these minorities, if they had the power to do so, the way Idi Amin did in Uganda ten years later when he expelled Asians including Ugandan citizens of Asian origin. Nyerere was the only African leader who publicly denounced Amin and called him a racist because of what he did.

Fortunately, there were no racial tensions in

Tanganyika after independence, earning the country a reputation as one of the most peaceful on the continent and tolerant of racial minorities.

But although the people celebrated independence and were glad to be masters of their own destiny as a nation, they did not see any dramatic improvement in their lives as many of them had expected.

Such changes don't come overnight, yet there were many people who had very high expectations, thinking that their lives would dramatically improve soon after the end of colonial rule. But that was not the case.

However, this was offset by the fact that there was a major achievement in one area, "overnight." The prophets of doom who had predicted racial conflict or some kind of civil strife soon after independence were proved wrong.

I remember a few years after independence that there were still some signs on toilets saying "Africans." I remember one very well at the bus station of the East African Railways & Harbours Corporation in Mbeya. No one took it down. It was simply ignored.

Although it reminded one of a bygone era and symbolized the subordinate status of Africans during colonial rule when they were not welcome in some places including a few hotels and clubs which had signs saying "Europeans," it did not inspire the kind of outrage - if any - some people might have expected from Africans after Tanganyika won independence.

There were Africans who simply accepted the status quo during colonial rule; there were those who simply ignored it; and there were, of course, those who were determined to change it.

But even those who sought changes in the status quo were no more hostile towards whites than those who did not after the country won independence. And that was one of the biggest achievements of the independence struggle, making it possible for people of all races to live in harmony.

Many whites who left Tanganyika after independence did so for economic reasons mainly because of the economic policies which deprived them of their property and even means of livelihood especially after the country adopted socialism in 1967 and not because they were targeted as whites.

Many Africans who owned a lot of land and even more than one house for rent also lost most of their property and were equally bitter because of such stringent measures designed, rightly or wrongly, to reduce income disparities and gaps between the rich and the poor in the quest for socialist transformation of the country.

It was the most ambitious exercise in social engineering in the history of post-colonial Africa launched only five years after Tanganyika won independence. But it also proved to be a disastrous failure in terms of economic development as the economy virtually came to a grinding halt in the mid- and late seventies, less than 10 years after the government enunciated its socialist policies embodied in the Arusha Declaration of February 1967.

Socialism and Africanization were some of the main reasons why many whites left or were forced to leave Tanganyika and later Tanzania.

When Tanganyika won independence in 1961, it had about 22,000 white settlers, mostly British; a significant number of Germans, some Dutch including Boers from South Africa and others. And Kenya had about 66,000 whites, mostly British including members of the British aristocracy, at independence in 1963. It also had a significant number of Boers, or Afrikaners, from South Africa who founded the town of Eldoret in the Western Highlands in the Great Rift Valley.

Robin Johnson, whom I mentioned earlier, was typical of the British settlers who had established themselves in East Africa, determined to make it their permanent home as civil servants working for the colonial government or as farmers or something else.

In fact, a significant number of them were born in Kenya or Tanganyika. Some came from South Africa and others from as far away as Australia and New Zealand. And many, or their children and grandchildren, are still there today in different parts Kenya and what is Tanzania today.

Some of the settlers who acquired large tracts of land were members of the British aristocracy, probably the last people who would think of relinquishing power to Africans one day. Johnson himself gave up his job as a civil servant and took up farming. He was the District Commissioner (D.C.) of Kongwa in the Central Province in Tanganyika during the ill-fated groundnut scheme that was intended to produce groundnuts on a commercial scale. The scheme was a disaster. He was later assigned to Arusha in northern Tanganyika, what was then called the Northern Province:

"Robin himself was becoming increasingly interested in Tanganyika's long-term future. He felt if he became a farmer, like his father before him, and thereby rooted in the soil, he could play a more permanent role in the country's development than permitted to a transitory civil servant.

He had met David Stirling, the founder of the Capricorn Africa Society, and felt that his policy of common citizenship and a multi-racial form of government might well be the answer for the East African states where Africans, though still backward, must soon begin to move politically, and there was a small settled European and Asian community.

He resigned from the Colonial Service in 1951 when he was alloted one of the Ol Molog farms [in Arusha in northern Tanganyika]. His colleagues thought he was quite mad. Surely every diligent Administrative Officer only had one goal in life - to be a Governor finally. How irresponsible of Robin carelessly to throw that chance

190

away."

Just as some white settlers were planning to turn East Africa into their permanent home dominated by whites, Africans were at the same time proceeding on a parallel path towards mobilization of political forces transcending race in their quest for independence and did not, for one moment, believe that the multiracial government proposed by some of the more liberal members of the settler community would ever include them as equal partners. And they spoke from experience.

The multiracial Legislative Councils, known as LEGCO, which existed during colonial rule were dominated by whites. And whatever was proposed by the colonial authorities for the future would have proceeded along the same lines. Universal adult suffrage, a cardinal principle cherished in every democratic society, was totally out of the question in this dispensation.

Many of the settlers were, of course, aware of the political awakening and agitation that was taking place but did not believe that the people of Kenya and Tanganyika would demand or win independence within a decade or so. Even some of the African leaders themselves said their countries would not win independence until the 1980s.

The British colonial office suggested that if independence ever came to Tanganyika, it would be in 1985. Britain had to have some kind of timetable - although only theoretically - since Tanganyika was not a typical colony, like Kenya, but a trusteeship territory under UN mandate, with Britain playing the role of "Big Brother" to guide the country towards independence on terms stipulated by the United Nations.

Yet the UN itself was not seriously concerned about freedom and independence for Africans without being pushed by African leaders who included Julius Nyerere as the pre-eminent African leader in Tanganyika.

In fact, political awakening among Africans had

191

already been going on for quite some time long before the "halcyon days" of colonial rule in the 1950s. And Julius Nyerere played a critical role at a very early age in galvanizing his colleagues into action, despite his humility. As Chief Abdallah Said Fundikira, who became one of the first cabinet members after independence, said about what type of person Nyerere was in those days: "If you want the truth, one did not particularly notice Nyerere."

He was talking about the time when Nyerere entered Makerere University College at the age of 22 after attending secondary school in Tabora, in western Tanganyika, the hometown of Fundikira, chief of the Nyamwezi tribe, one of the largest in Tanzania with more than one million people today.

It was when he was at Makerere that his leadership qualities came to be noticed when he formed the Tanganyika Welfare Association intended to help the small number of students from Tanganyika to work together as a collective entity for their own well-being. It was not a political organization but had the potential to become one.

The welfare association soon forged ties and eventually merged with the Tanganyika African Association (TAA), an organization founded by African civil servants in Tanganyika in 1929, to address their problems. But they had to operate within prescribed limits, as defined by the colonial authorities who said the association could only deal with welfare problems; nothing political.

Nyerere and his colleagues wanted the association to fight discrimination against the African civil servants who were being paid less than their European counterparts. It was a "welfare" problem, but with profound implications, hardly indistinguishable from political demands. He later described these "welfare" demands as "the politics of sheer complaints" which did not address the fundamental problem of inequity of power between Africans and

Europeans.

But he wanted the colonial authorities to pay attention to demands by Africans in order to bring about fundamental change in this asymmetrical relationship that had existed since the colonialists took over Tanganyika before he was born. As he recalled those days: "When I was born, there was not a single person who questioned why we were being ruled. And if my father had heard that we wanted changes, he would have asked me, 'What do you think you can do, you small silly boy?'"

But nothing could dissuade him from his commitment to justice, no matter what the cost. And much as his father would have been apprehensive of the situation, had he lived long enough to discuss the matter with his son after he became mature, Nyerere knew that nothing was going to change until Africans themselves did something to bring about change. His mother was equally apprehensive and probably even more so. She was quoted as saying:

"I began to know about Julius' activities when he was teaching at Pugu College [St. Francis College] in 1952. Everyday, a man called Dossa Aziz came to our house and he would talk with Julius for a long time.

One day I overheard them talking about taking over the government from Europeans.

I became afraid. Later I asked Julius if what I heard was true. When he said yes, I became more frightened. I told him what he was doing was bad. God had given him a good job and now he wanted to spoil it. But he said that what he was doing would benefit not only us but everyone in the country."

Nyerere had just returned to Tanganyika in October 1952 after three years at Edinburgh University in Scotland where he was admitted in October 1949. He earned a master's degree in economics and history, and also studied philosophy.

The fifties was a critical decade in the struggle for independence in Tanganyika. It was the decade when TANU (Tanganyika African National Union), the party that led Tanganyika to independence, was formed.

It was also the decade in which the colonial government tried to neutralize TANU, as much as the British colonial authorities tried to do to KANU (Kenya African National Union) in neighbouring Kenya when they arrested and imprisoned Jomo Kenyatta and other leaders in 1952 And it was the last decade of colonial rule in both colonies.

Before the 1958-1959 general election in Tanganyika, the British colonial government launched a harassment campaign to discredit and if possible destroy TANU. Nyerere was banned from making public speeches; he was accused of libel and put on trial; and twelve branches of TANU were closed down.

The banning of Nyerere came after a highly successful campaign across the country to get support for TANU and for his campaign for independence. He travelled to all parts of Tanganyika, to every province, in a battered Land Rover which belonged to his compatriot Dossa Aziz who gave the vehicle to TANU to help with the independence campaign, and was able to build, with his colleagues, the party's membership to unprecedented levels. Just within a year, TANU had 250,000 members.

It was during one of these campaign trips that I saw Nyerere for the first time when he came to address a mass rally in Tukuyu in the late 1950s; riding in the same Land Rover that had taken him to all parts of Tanganyika before.

I remember that day well. He wore a light green shirt and rode, standing, in the back of the Land Rover, waving at the crowd that had gathered to welcome him when he first arrived to address a mass rally at a football (soccer) field in Tukuyu one afternoon.

Although he was committed to non-violence, the

colonial authorities claimed that some of his speeches were highly inflammatory; but, to the people of Tanganyika, they were highly inspiring. And because of this he was banned, in early 1957, from making public speeches.

Yet he remained unperturbed. As he told a correspondent of *The New York Times* in Dar es Salaam, Tanganyika, on March 31, 1957: "I am a troublemaker, because I believe in human rights strongly enough to be one."

Earlier in the same year he had written an article published in the *Tanganyika Standard* which two district commissioners (D.Cs, as we called them, and as they also called themselves) complained about, claiming Nyerere had libelled them; twelve years later, I became a news reporter of the same newspaper.

Nyerere also said although TANU was committed to non-violence, the nationalist movement would resort to civil disobedience to achieve its goals; and, by implication, to violence if necessary, if there was no other option left in pursuit of independence. And his trial gave the colonial authorities the opportunity to learn more about him.

The trial was a turning point in the history of TANU and of the country as a whole. A reporter of *Drum* magazine was one of those who covered the trial. He had the following to say in the November 1958 edition when the proceedings took place in Dar es Salaam, the capital:

"The sun has not yet risen but hundreds of people are already gathered round the small courthouse in Dar es Salaam.

Some have come from distant villages, with blankets and cooking utensils as if for a camping holiday. They have been in Dar es Salaam for more than a week at the trial of the president of the Tanganyika African National Union (TANU), Julius Nyerere, on a charge of criminal libel. It was alleged that Nyerere wrote an article in which

195

two district commissioners were libelled.

Police constables line the streets round the court and a riot squad stands ready nearby in case of trouble. As the time draws near for the court to open, the crowds jostle and shove for the best positions.

The trial has been a mixture of exciting arguments, explosive surprises and hours of dullness.

Mr. Pritt - Nyerere's counsel - insisted that the two commissioners should be called to give evidence. He accused the government of prosecuting Nyerere without investigating his allegations. The government was telling the world that if anybody said anything against a district commissioner, he could be put into prison for saying what was true.

When Nyerere gave evidence, he took full responsibility for the article and said that he had written it to draw the attention of the government to certain complaints. He was followed by three witnesses who spoke of 'injustices' they had suffered at the hands of the the two district commissioners.

Halfway through the proceedings, the attorney-general appeared in court in person to announce on behalf of the Crown that it would not continue with the counts concerning one of the commissioners.

Now, on the last day of the show, the stars begin to arrive: Mr. Summerfield, the chief prosecutor; Mr. N.M. Rattansey, defence counsel who is assisting the famous British QC, Mr. D.N. Pritt. Mr. Nyerere, wearing a green bush shirt, follows later. He smiles and waves as members of the crowd cheer him.

The curtain goes up with the arrival of Mr. L.A. Davies, the magistrate. The court is packed. Everyone is tense and hushed.

The magistrate sums up then comes to judgement - Nyerere is found guilty!

The magistrate, in passing sentence, says he has formed the impression that Nyerere is an extremely intelligent and responsible man. He fines Nyerere Pounds 150 or six months. The money is raised by locals and the Kenya defence fund."

In the election that followed in 1958 - 1959, TANU won a landslide victory. It won 29 out of 30 seats in the general election. As Nyerere said after the victory, "Independence will follow as surely as the tick birds follow the rhino."

In March 1959, Sir Richard Turnbull, the last governor of Tanganyika, appointed to his 12-member cabinet five TANU members who had been elected to the Legislative Council (LEGCO), the colonial legislature which was established in 1926.

In 1958 Sir Richard Turnbull had succeeded Sir Edward Twining as governor of Tanganyika. He had previously served as chief colonial secretary in Kenya during the Emergency, which was during the Mau Mau uprising, and had witnessed first-hand the violence and bloodshed which resulted from the colonial government's refusal to address the grievances of the masses over land and working conditions and from its unwillingness to accept demands by Africans for freedom and independence. He did not want to see that happen in Tanganyika when he became governor.

Initially, the colonial government in Tanganyika wanted only three ministerial posts to be filled by LEGCO members, but Nyerere insisted on having a majority from his victorious party, TANU.

During the election, TANU had sponsored an Asian and a European for each seat, besides its own African candidates. The two also won.

Governor Turnbull conceded and appointed three Africans, one Asian and one European to the cabinet to represent TANU and the majority of the voters who had voted for TANU candidates.

It was also in the same month, March 1959, that

197

Nyerere was interviewed by *Drum* and spoke about the future of Tanganyika after it won independence, which was almost three years away:

"Tanganyika will be the first, most truly multiracial democratic country in Africa.

When we get our freedom, the light of a true multiracial democracy will be put high upon the top of the highest mountain, on Kilimanjaro, for all to see, particularly South Africa and America.

Tanganyika will offer the people of those countries free entry, without passports, to come and see real democracy at work.

As long as we do not have a popular government elected by the people on democratic principles, we will strive for freedom from any kind of domination.

We regard the [UN] Trusteeship as part of a scheme to keep Tanganyika under the British Crown indefinitely. The greatest enemy of our vision is the Colonial Office.

But Tanganyika cannot be freed by drawing up resolutions or by tabulating long catalogues of the evils of colonialism. Nor do we find it enough to tell rulers to quit Tanganyika. It will be freed only by action, and likewise the whole of Africa.

Continued colonialism is preventing investment in this country. Germany, for example, cannot invest money as long as the British are still here.

I agree that the country lacks technicians. So what? Shall we give the British another 40 years to train them? How many have they trained in the past 40 years?

As far as money for a self-governing Tanganyika is concerned, Tanganyika has not been receiving much money from the British taxpayer at all. For the past 11 years, Tanganyika has only received Pounds 9 million. I can raise 100 times that within a year if it becomes necessary.

I believe that the continued, not existence, but

citizenship of the European would be taken for granted had not the white man created a Kenya, a Central Africa [the Central African Federation of Rhodesia and Nyasaland], a South Africa and other similar places and situations.

African nationalism is not anti-white but simply anti-colonialist. When George Washington fought the imperialists, he was fighting for the divine right of Americans to govern themselves; he was not fighting colour.

The white man wants to live in Africa on his terms. He must dominate and be recognised by the rest of the inhabitants of this continent as their natural master and superior. But that we cannot accept. What we are after is fellow citizenship, and that is exactly what is frightening the white man.

The question is not whether we must get rid of whites, but whether they must get rid of themselves. Whites can no longer dominate in Africa. That dream is gone. Africa must be governed by Africans in the future.

Whether an immigrant African will have an equal part to play in this free Africa depends upon him and him alone. In Tanganyika, we are determined to demonstrate to the whole of Africa that democracy is the only answer.

We are being held back, not by local Europeans, but by the Colonial Office and, I believe, by Europeans in neighbouring countries, who are frightened of the possibility of success in Tanganyika."

A month later in April 1959, after the interview with *Drum*, Nyerere went to Zanzibar to attend a meeting of the Pan-African Freedom Movement of Eastern and Central Africa, popularly known as PAFMECA when I was growing up in Tanganyika, and of which he had previously been elected president.

One of the most prominent Tanganyikan leaders of PAFMECA was John Mwakangale from my home district,

Rungwe. He was also one of the TANU members who was elected as a member of the colonial legislature, LEGCO.

Mwakangale was also the leader who was assigned by the government of Tanganyika to receive Nelson Mandela in Mbeya when Mandela came to Tanganyika for the first time in 1962, soon after we won independence from Britain, as Mandela states in his book, *Long Walk to Freedom.*

While in Zanzibar, Nyerere played a critical role in forging unity between some Africans and some Arabs, bringing their political parties closer together in the struggle for independence and for the sake of national unity.

Speaking at a meeting of PAFMECA in Nairobi, Kenya, in September 1959, he made it clear that Europeans and Asians as well as others were welcome to remain in Africa as equal citizens after independence was achieved.

The following month, in October, he gave a speech in the Tanganyika colonial legislature (LEGCO) in which he uttered these famous words:

"We will light a candle on mount Kilimanjaro which will shine beyond our borders, giving hope where there is despair, love where there is hate, and dignity where before there was only humiliation."

In December 1959, Britain's new Colonial Secretary Ian McLeod announced that Tanganyika would be given virtual home rule towards the end of 1960 under a constitution that would guarantee an African majority in the colonial legislature, LEGCO. However, Nyerere criticized the retention of income and literacy qualifications as eligibility criteria for voters and for membership in the legislature.

He was also critical of the reservation of a specific number of seats in LEGCO for the European and Asian

200

minorities. But he saw the concessions by the British colonial rulers, including new constitutional provisions guaranteeing a legislature with an African majority, as a step towards independence in the not-so-distant future.

In the elections of August 1960, TANU again won by a landslide, 70 out of 71 seats, its biggest victory so far and less than a year before independence.

Nyerere was sworn in as chief minister of government under a new constitution, but the governor, Sir Richard Turnbull, continued to hold certain veto powers, although rarely exercised, if at all, since it was now inevitable that Tanganyika would soon be independent.

Nyerere's status as the leader of Tanganyika was formally acknowledged even outside the colony, for example, when he attended a meeting of British Commonwealth prime ministers in London in March 1961, although Tanganyika was still not independent.

But in his capacity as prime minister of Tanganyika since the colony won internal self-government, hence *de facto* head of government in lieu of the governor, he joined other African leaders in denouncing the apartheid regime of South Africa and its racist policies and declared that if South Africa remained a member of the Commonwealth, Tanganyika would not join the Commonwealth; a position he had articulated earlier in August 1960 when he said: "To vote South Africa in, is to vote us out."

South Africa withdrew from the Commonwealth, and many people attribute this to Nyerere's uncompromising stand on the apartheid regime and his threat to keep Tanganyika out of the Commonwealth had South Africa remained a member.

Following a constitutional conference in March 1961, Colonial Secretary Ian McLeod announced that Tanganyika would have internal self-government on May 1, and full independence in December in the same year.

On 9 December 1961, Tanganyika became independent. A few days later, it was unanimously accepted as the 104th member of the United Nations. Nyerere was 39 years old and, at that time, the youngest national leader in the world.

On 9 January 1962, Nyerere resigned as prime minister and appointed Rashidi Kawawa, minister without portfolio, as his successor. He said he resigned to rebuild the party which had lost its focus and to give the country a new purpose now that independence had been won.

But with independence came responsibilities. It was no easy task. So much lay ahead.

Appendix II:

Reprinted with permission from Godfrey Mwakikagile, *Kenya: Identity of A Nation*, First Edition, New Africa Press, 2007, pp. 224 – 233.

The Swahili People
and Swahili Culture

THE Swahili are found mostly in Kenya and Tanzania along the coast. They are also found in urban centres in other parts of both countries but not in large numbers as they are in the coastal regions. And they are mostly Muslim.

The contrast is sometimes glaring. For example, when I was growing up in Rungwe District in the Southern Highlands of Tanganyika, later Tanzania, there was not a single mosque in the town of Tukuyu, the district headquarters, or in the entire district. And there were very few Muslims, only a handful, mostly in Tukuyu.

But it was an entirely different story along the coast and in many other urban centres in the country.

Although the Swahili people, or Waswahili as they are known in the Kiswahili language, are considered to be de-tribalised Africans, members of tribes indigenous to the coast are also considered to be Waswahili.

One of the best examples are the Zaramo, or Wazaramo, in Tanzania who are the original inhabitants of Dar es Salaam (formerly known as Mzizima when it was a village), the former capital which is now the commercial centre although in most cases it is still the capital city of Tanzania. Even the president of Tanzania still lives in Dar es Salaam, not in Dodoma, in the hinterland, which is the official capital.

The Swahili have lived along the coast for centuries, probably since 100 A.D.

There were African tribes along the coast, and when the Arabs came, they interacted and intermarried with the indigenous people. The product of this intermingling was the Swahili people and Swahili culture.

Therefore most of the people who are called Swahili or Waswahili are a mixed group of people, racially with the Arabs, and in terms of inter-tribal marriage of coastal tribes who were from the beginning strongly influenced by the Arabs and adopted Islam and Arab culture.

Persians, especially in what is Tanzania today, also contributed to the evolution of the Swahili people and the Swahili culture. They came mostly from a region called Shiraz in Persia, now Iran, and their descendants who intermarried with Africans still live in Zanzibar today. They are also found in other parts of Tanzania and even in Kenya.

But marriage between Arabs and Africans, and between Persians and Africans, was one-sided in the sense that it was Arab men and Persian men who married black African women or kept them as concubines. It was unthinkable for African men to marry Arab women or Persian women. And the intermarriage was mostly between Arabs and Africans. Persians who settled in East Africa were far fewer than the Arabs who migrated to the region through the centuries.

What is also important to remember is that there was no Islam before the prophet Mohammed. Yet there were Arabs who settled in East Africa long before Islam became a religion, and long before Mohammed was born.

Therefore evolution of Swahili culture - a product of intermingling and intermarriage between Arabs and Africans - started long before the advent and propagation of Islam. But it was reinforced centuries later with the spread of the Islamic faith. And the Swahili people themselves came into being before Islam since racial intermarriage between Arabs and Africans started taking place centuries before Islam became a religion.

It was not until the 700s A.D. that Islam was introduced to East Africa after prophet Mohammed died in 632 A.D. It was also during that period that Arabs started settling in East Africa in large numbers, many of them spreading the Islamic faith.

But while Swahilisation of the East African coast and evolution of the Swahili culture preceded Islam, Islam did, centuries later especially since the 700s A.D., profoundly influence Swahili culture and in fact virtually transformed it into Islamic culture, clearly demonstrated even today on the East African coast where almost all the Swahili people are Muslims, or Moslems, whichever term they prefer to use.

What is also important to remember is that it was not just those who were the product of inter-racial marriage between Arabs and Africans who became or were considered to be Swahili people together with de-tribalised Africans and tribal Africans who had adopted Swahili culture. Arabs themselves also became Swahili, or Waswahili, just like their black counterparts and those of mixed race.

Even today, Arabs in Kenya and Tanzania are called - and consider themselves to be - Waswahili. The Swahili identity transcends race.

Most of the Arabs in Kenya and Tanzania speak Swahili, or Kiswahili, as their mother-tongue although they are also bilingual and speak Arabic as well.

Even many Swahili people who have African and Arab ancestry also speak Arabic although Kiswahili is their native language as much as it is for de-tribalised black Africans who don't know their tribal languages.

Tanzania has more people whose mother-tongue is Kiswahili than Kenya does. But Kenya also has some Waswahili, especially those in Mombasa and Lamu, who are more "typical Swahili" than many Swahili people in Tanzania.

One of them is renowned Kenyan scholar, Professor Ali Mazrui from Mombasa, who is both black African and Arab in terms of racial heritage, as many people along the East African coast are. As he has emphatically stated on a number of occasions, Kiswahili is his mother-tongue, or his native language. But he also speaks Arabic. And he is a Muslm.

He is a typical Swahili – in spite of being Westernised in terms of education and lifestyle – and has the following to say about the Swahili people and the Swahili culture in one of his lectures:

Uswahili International:
Between Language and Cultural Synthesis

Professor Ali A. Mazrui

Delivered at Fort Jesus, Mombasa, Kenya, on 19 July 2005, as part of the launch of the Swahili Resource Centre, Coastal Branch, Kenya.

The event was also a commemoration of the works of Sheikh Al-Amin Ali Mazrui, the late Chief Kadhi of Kenya who was also the father of the future professor, Ali Amin Mazrui, who was 14 years old when his father died in 1947 at the age of 58.

This Resource Centre is primarily focused on Swahili culture, rather than the Swahili language.

Is there a Swahili culture apart from the language? A culture is a way of life of a people.

In order for there to be a distinct Swahili culture, there has to be a distinct Swahili people. Is there a Swahili people with a distinct way of life of its own?

The Swahili people are those who originated the Swahili language. They themselves emerged at the Coast of Kenya and Tanzania; they were originally overwhelmingly Muslim and they had strong cultural links with Coastal African tribes, on the one hand, and the Arabian peninsular, on the other.

Like medieval Islam, Swahili culture was enhanced by a spirit of *creative synthesis*. Islamic civilization was at its best when it was prepared to learn from other cultures and civilizations.

In mathematics ancient Islamic civilization was stimulated by India. In philosophy Islamic civilization was stimulated by ancient Greeks. In architecture Islamic civilization was stimulated by pre-Islamic Persia. In asylum and political refuge early Muslims enjoyed the protection of Africans in the Horn of Africa.

During the lifetime of the Prophet Muhammad himself, Arab Muslims were being persecuted by pre-Islamic Arabs on the Arabian peninsular. A group of endangered Arab Muslims crossed the Red Sea into Abyssinia (now called Ethiopia) in search of political asylum and religious refuge.

They were protected by an African Christian monarch. Among the refugees was Uthman bin Affan, later destined to become the third Caliph of Islam and the protector of the Qur'an.

Islamic civilization subsequently declined when it became less and less ready to learn from other civilizations, and condemned major cultural changes as bid'a - that is, as dangerous innovations.

Like ancient Islamic civilization, Swahili culture initially prospered through a spirit of *creative synthesis* – ready to learn from other cultures.

While the basic foundation of the Kiswahili language was Bantu African, the language quite early demonstrated readiness to borrow extensively from Arabic.

Sometimes the configuration of Arabic and Bantu African concepts constituted a remarkable balancing act.

Bantu:
Kusini na Kaskazini – North and South
Arabic:
Mashariki na Magharibi – East and West
Bantu:
Uchumi – Economics
Arabic:
Siasa – Politics
Bantu:
Bunge – Parliament
Arabic:
Raisi – President
Bantu:
Balozi – Ambassador
Arabic:
Waziri – Minister
Bantu:
Chumvi (or Munyu) – Salt
Arabic:
Sukari – Sugar

Bantu:
Mungu – God

Arabic:
Angel – Malaika

Bantu:
Nguvu – Strength
Arabic:
Afya – Health
Bantu:
Utumwa – Slavery
Arabic:
Uhuru – Freedom
Bantu:
Mjomba – Maternal Uncle
Arabic:
Ami – Paternal Uncle
Bantu:
Shangazi – Paternal Aunt
Arabic:
Khalati – Maternal Aunt
Bantu:
Nyama – Meat
Arabic:
Samaki – Fish
Bantu:
Mto – River
Arabic:
Bahari – Ocean or Sea
Bantu:
Moja, Mbili, Tatu. Nne, Tano – One, Two, Three, Four, Five
Arabic:
Sita, Saba, Tisa – Six, Seven, Nine

Bantu:
Kumi – Ten
Arabic:
Ishirini mpaka Mia – Twenty to a Hundred.

In interacting with both Arab and Indian civilizations, Swahili architecture and systems of decoration were affected.

Elaborately carved Lamu doors, copper decorated chests, ivory decorated Lamu thrones, entered Swahili decorative worlds – as well as beautiful copper coffee pots and the small coffee cups.

In the creative synthesis Swahili culture helped to Africanize the tabla (Indian drum) for events which have ranged from tarabu (Swahili concert) to maulidi (celebrating the Prophet's birthday), alongside matari (dancing drums with small bells attached).

Arabic music also provided the ud to Swahili culture – an Arabian Nights guitar.

The Swahili flute was influenced by both Middle Eastern and South Asian orchestration.

Creative synthesis also incorporated into Kiswahili several food cuisines. Swahili cuisine seeks to incorporate such South Asian dishes as pilau, biriani, and chapatti – none of which are identical with the Indian varieties.

Some of the spices carry Arab names rather than Indian – such as bizari for curry powder and thumu or thomo for garlic.

Swahili architecture in places like Lamu and the ruins of Gedi continue to reflect this responsiveness to the cultures of other societies.

This Fort Jesus was built by the Portuguese. It was from time to time Swahilized, especially when the rulers of Mombasa were for a while either Swahilized Arabs or Arabized Waswahili.

The Portuguese brought maize to East Africa. Most

Europeans at the time called maize "Indian corn".

The word "Indian" refers to Americo-Indians (Red Indians, rather than Hindustan).

To the present day, the name for maize in Kiswahili is hindi (singular) or mahindi (plural). A salute to Montezuma, the Emperor of Mexico.

Words we have borrowed from Portuguese include the big one – pesa, meaning money. It is borrowed from pesos, the Iberian currency.

Other Portuguese words: sapatu (slippers), shimizi (female undergarment), kandirinya (water kettle).

The Germans gave Kiswahili such educational words as shule (school). The Arabs gave us elimu (scholarly knowledge), the Africans gave us chuo and chuo kikuu (educational institution and university), and the British gave us words which range from profesa to sayansi, from baiskeli to dimokrasi, and from manuwari (man of war – or battleship) to sinema (cinema).

This readiness to respond to other cultures and languages makes Kiswahili very similar to the English language. Both languages have been spectacularly successful. English words which the British have borrowed from Arabic include algebra, tariff (from taarifa), admiral (from emir), and, surprisingly, alcohol (al-quhl).

The most famous English loan word borrowed from Kiswahili is the word safari. In English the word means "hunting trip in Africa" – though in Swahili usage safari refers to any kind of travelling.

Kiswahili borrowed the word from Arabic and then loaned the word to the English language. *Creative synthesis* in all its intricate interconnections.

We must conclude that although the Swahili language is the legacy of words, the Swahili culture is a much wider phenomenon – including marriage customs, the traditions of child rearing, cuisine, architecture, dress code.

Kiswahili has greatly influenced neighboring African

languages. The kanzu in Kenya is associated with Swahili culture, and most wearers of the kanzu in Kenya are Muslims.

The kanzu in Uganda is not associated with any religion. The Kabaka of Buganda – a leading member of the Anglican global community – often wears the kanzu on ceremonial Christian occasions.

The word for religion in Luganda is dini. "Dini" also serves the same purpose in a large number of other East African indigenous languages.

Today we start an enterprise about Swahili culture as a whole. We have also honored Sheikh Al-Amin Aly Mazrui because he was one of the most influential writers of the Swahili language and a major expert of the manners, customs and beliefs of the Waswahili.

May this enterprise be blessed by our ancestors, supported by our people, served by our community, protected by our government and helped to grow to full maturity and triumph by the Almighty God. Amen.

Kila tunapomsheherekea mtu mwema, huwa na sisi tuna wema ndani ya nyoyo zetu.

An American playwright [John Drinkwater] has captured the same spirit in the following words about Abraham Lincoln:

When the high heart we magnify,
And the sure vision celebrate,
And worship greatness passing by,
Ourselves are great.

On a day like this I am proud and grateful that my father's high heart has been magnified, his sure vision celebrated, and his greatness suitably recognized.

212

Appendix III:

Tanzania in A Capsule

Tanzania's ancient roots long predate modern colonialism.

It was one of the first regions of the world known to have been inhabited by our earliest ancestors and the footprints of three humans at Laetoli in the north of the country have been carbon dated as being almost four million years old.

The footprints are located near Olduvai Gorge which is known as "The Cradle of Mankind" where the remains of many prehistoric humans, tools and animals have been excavated.

Coastal Tanzania, and notably the city of Kilwa, was to play a prominent role in the trade in gold, ivory and slaves from the African interior while Zanzibar, which traces its history back for many centuries, was a major pre-colonial trading point.

Set just south of the equator, the snow-capped Mount

Kilimanjaro is 5,895 metres (19,650 feet) and Africa's highest point.

In 1885, as a result of the "scramble for Africa" by European colonial powers, mainland Tanzania (Tanganyika) was declared a German protectorate known as Deutsch-Ostafrika (German East Africa).

The Maji Maji (Swahili for "water water") rebellion of 1905/6, involving peasants in the southern part of the country, challenged German rule.

The uprising, caused by the Germans forcing smallholder farmers in the south of the country to grow cotton, was brutally put down by the Germans with as many as 300,000 people estimated to have been killed.

Defeated in Europe in the First World War, Germany was forced to surrender the territory in 1919 to Britain as a protectorate under the League of Nations, the forerunner of the United Nations (UN). In 1947, Tanganyika was placed under the UN Trusteeship Council. It was still administered by Britain.

The Tanganyika African Association (TAA) was formed in 1929 as the country's earliest organised political protest movement. It sought greater African participation in government where Africans were discriminated against in favor of whites for appointments to senior posts.

In 1953, Julius Kambarage Nyerere, the son of a minor chief from the northwest of the country and a secondary school teacher, was elected its leader. In July 1954, he became a founder and was elected as the first president of the Tanganyika African National Union (TANU) which replaced TAA.

In 1955, faced with the choice between teaching and politics, Nyerere chose the latter.

TANU won Tanganyika's first general election in September 1958 which elected Nyerere as a Member of Parliament. He was unopposed in the 1960 elections after which he became Chief Minister.

In the 1960 elections, TANU won 70 of the 71 seats in

the National Assembly. The single seat the party did not win was won by a loyal TANU member who opposed the official candidate and who immediately joined the TANU ranks after his victory thereby making Tanganyika a *de facto* one party state under British colonial rule even before independence.

Self Government

Tanganyika became self-governing in May 1961 with Nyerere as Prime Minister. But six weeks after independence, Nyerere resigned as premier to work on bridging the potential gap between TANU and the elected government.

He was succeeded by Rashidi Kawawa. A year later on Republic Day (9 December 1962), Nyerere became Tanganyika's first President with Kawawa as his deputy.

Nyerere shaped Tanzania and his legacy lives on well after his retirement in 1985 as president of the country and five years later as official leader of the ruling party.

He united the country's more than 120 tribes who use the common national language, Swahili (the world's seventh most spoken language), thereby overcoming potential ethnic and religious divides.

Beyond that, the country has enjoyed internal peace since independence while the union with Zanzibar and Tanzania's unrivaled support for liberation movements fighting to rid southern Africa of minority rule, remain Nyerere's and Tanzania's most enduring legacies.

Ali Hassan Mwinyi was elected as Tanzania's second post-independence president and Benjamin William Mkapa as its third.

Under the constitution, the presidents of Tanzania and Zanzibar are now limited to two five-year terms in office. A further constraint on incumbents is that presidents must choose their Cabinet from elected Members of Parliament and they can no longer nominate outsiders to fill these jobs.

Zanzibar

Zanzibar was declared a British protectorate in 1890 as part of the European "scramble for Africa".

The British politically and economically favoured the Arab minority (the second largest ruling minority in Africa after South Africa's whites) placing the Sultan and his Arab government in power at independence.

Thirty-three days later the Zanzibar Revolution occurred. This brought to power the Afro-Shirazi Party (ASP) led by Sheikh Abeid Amani Karume.

In the pre-independence elections the ASP had won 54.21 per cent of the popular vote. But, as a result of constitutional gerrymandering by the British and Arabs, it won only 13 of the 31 elected seats.

The union between Tanganyika and Zanzibar followed three-and-a-half months later on 26 April 1964 with the unified sovereign states now known as Tanzania.

Under the articles of union both countries retained a degree of sovereignty with their own presidents, governments and responsibility for specified domestic affairs.

Other areas such as foreign affairs, defense and security became union subjects.

Nyerere was elected as President of Tanzania, Karume the First Vice-President and Kawawa the Second Vice-President.

In February 1977, TANU and the ASP merged to form the Chama Cha Mapinduzi (Revolutionary Party) with Nyerere as its chairman.

Ujamaa

In January 1967, Tanzania adopted a policy of Ujamaa (self-reliance) under the Arusha Declaration. This was widely known as a brand of "African socialism" which endeavored to eliminate poverty, ignorance and disease through community participation.

The declaration also enshrined party supremacy over parliament. However, the shift to a multi-party constitution on 1 July 1992 automatically restored the British-based supremacy of parliament.

There is no constitutional restriction on Parliament's authority. The role of the courts is to enforce the laws Parliament passes and all other law-making bodies in the country such as councils exercise their powers to make by-laws, through the authorisation of Parliament.

Recent Political Developments

The growth of multi-party democracy in Tanzania, in common with other countries in the region, is inhibited by the weakness of the opposition.

Power struggles and bickering beset opposition politics further undermining their weak power base and they rarely offer new faces or policies to arrest Tanzania's economic and social malaise and inequalities.

In the rural areas, where 85 per cent of the population lives, the CCM structures remain virtually unchallenged even though only the more strident voices of the urban minority are heard by the media and donors.

Election results are routinely challenged in the courts as being "rigged" by government and there is an unwillingness to accept defeat which is an inherent component of any democracy.

Tanzania's constitutional debate, and those in other countries throughout the region, offers a classic insight into opposition politics.

Few (government or opposition supporters) question the need for constitutional amendments which were mooted well before opposition politics were legalised. But the underlying assumption remains that anything advocated by government is suspect and should be automatically challenged.

On 24 April 1998, the government proposed a "White Paper" which would allow everyone to express their views on possible constitutional change. Automatically this proposal was rejected by the opposition.

With the next presidential and parliamentary elections scheduled for the year 2000, the government may have little choice but to proceed alone thereby leading to further domestic opposition and external protest.

Tanzania today is a multi-party democracy with 13 legally registered political parties, five of whom have places in Parliament.

The CCM remains the dominant political force winning 186 of the 232 (182 mainland, 50 Zanzibar) elected Parliamentary seats in the 1995 elections. A further 24 were won by Civil United Front (CUF), 16 by the National Conference for Construction and Reform (NCCR-Mageuzi), and three each by the Party for Democratic Development (CHADEMA) and the United Democratic Party (UDP).

The other parties did not win any seats. A further 36 seats in Parliament are nominated, one reserved for the disabled and the remainder for women, thereby ensuring they are better represented in the nation's legislative body.

There were three major elements in the 1995 elections, one of which continues to haunt Tanzania.

All candidates ran on an anti-corruption ticket and this issue dominated questions during campaign rallies, reflecting the public's disquiet.

Secondly, a regional voting bloc emerged. The WaChagga from Kilimanjaro voted overwhelmingly for their home candidate (Augustine Mrema) in the presidential election and for the NCCR party.

Regional politics, common elsewhere in southern Africa, were a new experience for Tanzanians, making the elections in the year 2000 an important test as to the nation's cohesiveness.

There are fears that the longer term issue involving Zanzibar and the ongoing political stalemate on the islands could have repercussions on the mainland.

CUF continues to dispute the outcome of the 1995 elections in which the CCM Presidential candidate, Salmin Amour, was awarded a narrow majority over his rival.

This result, CUF insists, was rigged, a charge denied by the CCM.

Several major western aid donors are perceived as supporting CUF while the Commonwealth and several other bodies have sought a solution to the impasse which has resulted in elected CUF members boycotting sessions of the island's House of Representatives.

Theoretically, President Amour is serving his final term but there are pressures on Zanzibar for him to abrogate the constitution and stand again. A decision to do so would threaten the Union.

Governance

After the 1967 Arusha Declaration, Tanzania saw the pre-eminence of the ruling party in all matters relating to governance as well as in running the socio-economic affairs and the political direction of the nation.

Now the constitution decentralises that role establishing local government authorities and prescribing their roles and functions.

Tanzania is trying to attain good governance through instilling managerial and organisational efficiency, accountability, legitimacy, responsiveness to public aspirations and needs, transparency and pluralism.

There are, however, a number of structural and managerial distortions (such as the civil service) which have been recognised as deep-rooted causes of inefficiencies in the area of governance.

Under President Mkapa, the country is committed to continuing the trend towards more openness, greater freedom of choice for the individual and the emergence of institutions of governance committed to the needs and aspirations of Tanzanians.

Gender

The government has been striving to promote decision-making that benefits all social groups.

However, despite all the measures taken to bring about gender equality and equity, girls and women are still a disadvantaged group.

Women lag behind in every sector, be it access to education and training, health, or to means of production such as land and credit as well as formal employment and participation in structures of power, including decision-making.

Women participation in governance, politics and decision-making has, however, been increasing. Women MPs now constitute 15 per cent of all legislators, up from 11 per cent in 1985.

Women in government form 9 per cent of the total. Thirty-six seats in Parliament are reserved for women and, while in some western circles such legislation attracts criticism, the decision is defended by Tanzanian leaders on the grounds that without such a system fewer women would have Parliamentary seats.

Efforts to empower women in decision-making, politics, governance and socio-economic activities include enhancing women's legal capacity, women's economic empowerment as well as improvement of their access to education, training and employment.

The National Women in Development Policy of 1992 provides for all social actors as far as gender and development are concerned.

Legal Status

The constitution of the United Republic of Tanzania provides equal rights for both men and women.

However, there is still some legislation that tends to undermine the welfare of women, especially with regard to inheritance and access to means of production such as land.

The government is reviewing these laws in a bid to improve the welfare of women.

Moreover, in an attempt to protect women and children against widespread sexual offences, the Sexual Offences Special Provisions Act came into force on 1 July 1998. Zanzibar is also introducing similar legislation.

In 1985, Tanzania introduced a Bill of Rights to guarantee the freedoms of all Tanzanians.

In 1992, the Nyalali Commission had found 40 laws inconsistent with the rights inherent in the constitution. These laws were adjudged by the Nyalali Commission as "bad laws", some unconstitutional and other outdated.

The Law Reform Commission has already reviewed 28 of the 40 laws. Now the Attorney-General must present proposed amendments to Parliament.

The remaining 12 laws fall under Zanzibar's ministry responsible for Justice and Constitutional Affairs.

Civil Society

Until 1982, the government was perceived as the nations provider.

The global economic crisis of the 1980s was among other factors which forced the government to shed some of these social responsibilities as well as disengage from the direct running of socio-economic activities.

This left room for the growth of the civil society as manifested by the proliferation of non-governmental organisations (NGOs) and community-based organisations (CBOs), some of whom are trying to cultivate development from the grassroots.

Human Rights Commission

There are currently moves towards the formation of a Human Rights Commission in Tanzania.

This follows a decision to that effect announced in the National Assembly during the 1996/97 and 1998/99 budget sessions by the Minister of Justice and Constitutional Affairs.

Media

The Tanzanian government encourages the growth of a "responsible" press.

In recent years private newspapers, magazines and television stations have mushroomed.

The Media Council of Tanzania was registered on 22 May 1997 after being formed at a mass media general convention on 28 June 1995.

This is an independent NGO established by journalists, publishers and media service-oriented organisations to foster and maintain freedom of the media.

Local Administration

For administrative purposes, the United Republic of Tanzania is divided into 26 regions (provinces) - 21 on mainland Tanzania and five on Zanzibar.

Regional Impact

Tanzania, given its economic and geographical realities, is caught on the horns of a dilemma in post-apartheid southern Africa and the factors which determine its direction are often misunderstood.

As the northernmost Southern African Development Community (SADC) state it is somewhat peripheral to the regional grouping it championed.

Rather, its focus is closer to home: on the Great Lakes area (it provides sanctuary to 300,000 refugees from those areas of conflict) and the restoration of the defunct East African Community (Kenya, Tanzania and Uganda).

Its political stability and prevailing peace, lack of internal ethnic tensions, and the respect in which it is held, offer important prospects for regional peace-making which can be tedious, time-consuming and fraught with potential misunderstanding.

Its peaceful transition to multi-party democracy is an example for the region.

Source: Democracy Factfile – Tanzania – SD – SARDC www.sardc.net/SD/sd_factfile_tanzania.htm

Appendix IV:

Nyerere and Nkrumah on Continental Union under one Government

Excerpts from Bill Sutherland and Matt Mayer, *Guns and Gandhi in Africa: Pan African Insight on Nonviolence, Armed Struggle and Liberation in Africa,* Africa World Press, 2000.

Julius K. Nyerere:

My differences with Kwame were that Kwame thought there was somehow a shortcut, and I was saying that there was no shortcut. This is what we have inherited, and we'll have to proceed within the limitations that that inheritance has imposed on us.

Kwame thought that somehow you could say, "Let there be a United States of Africa" and it would happen. I kept saying, "Kwame, it's a slow process."

He had tremendous contempt for a large number of leaders of Africa and I said, "Fine, but they are there. What are you going to do with them? They don't believe as you do – as you and I do – in the need for the unity of Africa. BUT WHAT DO YOU DO? THEY ARE THERE, AND WE HAVE TO PROCEED ALONG WITH EVERYBODY!"

And I said to him in so many words that we're not going to have an African Napoleon, who is going to conquer the continent and put it under one flag. It is not possible.

At the OAU conference in 1963, I was actually trying to defend Kwame. I was the last to speak and Kwame had said this charter has not gone far enough because he thought he would leave Addis with a United States of Africa.

I told him that this was absurd; that it can't happen. This is what we have been able to achieve. No builder, after putting the foundation down, complains that the building is not yet finished. You have to go on building and building until you finish; but he was impatient because he saw the stupidity of the others.

Bill Sutherland:

You said that you and Nkrumah had one objective, but you differed on how to achieve it. When you thought about a united Africa, did you think that the present nation-states would emerge?

Nyerere:

When I clashed with Kwame, it was when we were very close to a federation of East African states and Kwame was completely opposed to the idea.

He said that regionalization - that's what he called it - was Balkanization on a larger scale.

I said "Look, Kwame, this is absurd." I thought that historically there were grounds for different groupings of countries trying to come together. West Africans at one

226

one time – under the British – had a common currency. Basically, the French had two huge colonies – French Equatorial Africa and French West Africa. I thought it was possible to move towards unity by putting those areas together. But even that didn't happen.

I thought that these groups could come together naturally, within the OAU. Then there could be propaganda, an incentive, and the push for greater unity. Kwame thought that we all could just sit down together and come out as a United States of Africa.

I think that Kwame was perhaps over-influenced by the way the US and the Soviet Union came together. You know the way the thirteen colonies came together, drafted a charter, and then declared the United States of America. I never thought it would work this way, because these African countries had become independent and the mistake was evident in East Africa.

If we wanted to come together, we should have come together before independence, because if you wait until after independence it cannot be done. With four presidents, four flags, four national anthems, four seats at the UN - ahh! It's extremely difficult!

Sutherland:

Didn't you note, about the preamble of the OAU, that it says "We the heads of state" - it doesn't even say "We the People?"

Nyerere:

No, what I said was that the UN Charter has its better: it says "We the People of the world," whereas the OAU Charter says "We the heads of state."

Sutherland:

Did you not, at a certain time, just shake your head and say that there must be a devil in Africa?

Nyerere:

I said that there is a devil in Africa.

I went to Addis and it was an incredible meeting. Here is this continent of young nations coming from

227

colonialism and so forth and the debate is awful, and really what provoked me was the French-speaking countries, you know.

With all their French culture, training in rationalization – you can't really argue with those fellows.

And I discovered some of these fellows have their visas – *their visas* – signed by the French ambassadors in their own countries! And I said, "Oh, but I thought you were fighting for freedom?"

I had given up PAFMECA [Pan-African Freedom Movement of East and Central Africa].

PAFMECA was 1962, and in '63 the North African and the West African countries had divided themselves between the Casablanca group and the Monrovia group, the radicals and conservatives – really absurd!

So I welcomed the idea that we could all be together, rather than have a continent divided along ideological lines.

After the OAU was established in 1963, I allowed PAFMECA to die out. I'm still quietly complaining, because PAFMECA was a movement of people. It was an organization of the liberation movements, and therefore could be a movement of people.

"We the heads of state!" When I hear the African heads of state talking like a bunch of colonials sent by France, of course I get livid! That's why I said there is a devil in Africa, and that devil is still around. We are still fighting that blessed devil!

CPSIA information can be obtained at www.ICGtesting.com
Printed in the USA
LVOW10s1112140515

438505LV00001B/82/P

9 789987 930838